A ROMANO-BRITISH AND MEDIEVAL SETTLEMENT SITE AT STOKE ROAD, BISHOP'S CLEEVE, GLOUCESTERSHIRE EXCAVATIONS IN 1997

by Dawn Enright and Martin Watts

with contributions by
Jane Bircher, Nigel Cameron, Christopher Dyer, Rowena Gale, Peter Guest,
Emma Harrison, Julie Jones, Jacqueline McKinley, Mark Maltby, Quita Mould,
Fiona Roe, Chris Salter, David Smith, Jane Timby, Graeme Walker and Keith Wilkinson

COTSWOLD ARCHAEOLOGY

Bristol and Gloucestershire Archaeological Report No. 1

By agreement with Cotswold Archaeology this report is distributed free
to members of the Bristol and Gloucestershire Archaeological Society
To accompany Volume 120 of the Society's *Transactions* for 2002

BRISTOL AND GLOUCESTERSHIRE ARCHAEOLOGICAL REPORT NO. 1

© Authors and Cotswold Archaeological Trust Ltd, 2002
Headquarters Building, Unit 9, Kemble Business Park, Cirencester, Glos. GL7 6BQ

All rights reserved. No part of this publication may be reproduced, stored in a retrieval system, or transmitted in any form or by any means electronic, photocopying, recording or otherwise without the prior permission of Cotswold Archaeological Trust Ltd.

ISSN 1479-2389
ISBN 0 9523196 6 7
Cotswold Archaeological Trust Ltd
Headquarters Building,
Unit 9, Kemble Business Park
Cirencester, Glos. GL7 6BQ

Series Editor: Martin Watts
Produced by Cotswold Archaeological Trust Ltd, Cirencester
Printed by Trio Graphics Ltd, Gloucester

FOREWORD

It gives me great pleasure, as Chairman both of the Bristol and Gloucestershire Archaeological Society's Publications Committee and of its Council, to write a foreword to the first report in this exciting co-operation with Cotswold Archaeology.

The Society has, for well over a century, sought not only to promote the study of the history and archaeology of the region but also to provide a means for disseminating the results of such work. The *Transactions* have, quite rightly, acquired and maintained the highest reputation in achieving this aim. Increasingly, however, the constraints of space have delayed and even inhibited the appearance of some reports of appropriate quality and great interest, thereby increasing the already large backlog of material awaiting publication.

The Society, therefore, welcomes this venture. We are delighted by the publication of this report, which we hope will inaugurate a series, to stand alongside the *Transactions*. We are pleased to assist with prompt publication so that what has been learned can assist others to understand better their own current work. We are confident that this collaboration offers both a considerable benefit to our members and an appropriate way for Cotswold Archaeology to disseminate the outcomes of some of its important local activities.

Professor Michael Oakeshott
Chairman of the Bristol and Gloucestershire Archaeological Society
October 2002

PUBLISHING ARCHAEOLOGY: THE COTSWOLD ARCHAEOLOGY APPROACH

Archaeological investigations of all kinds produce information and data that deserve wide circulation and general access if they are ever to be used for the ultimate purpose of reconstructing something of our ancient past. However, as the number and diversity of investigations increase, so too does the burden of disseminating archaeological results. This is not a new problem. Committees and working groups have addressed the issue at regular intervals over the last 25 years or more, and every time come up with slightly different responses as the nature of the information to be communicated changes and the technical means by which information can be carried develops. With more than 7000 investigations a year happening in England alone the problem is arguably more urgent now than it has ever been, and the technology to solve it more diverse than ever. What we need are new solutions to an old and familiar problem.

Some archaeologists dream of a day when the results of all excavations and fieldwork projects will appear on the Internet and be accessible to all at the touch of a button from the comfort of an arm-chair or office desk. And certainly that day is coming for all of us if today's techno-wizards are to be believed. For some it is already here of course, but not everyone has easy access to a computer and many would rather sit in their arm-chair with a glass of beer and a good old-fashioned book than be clicking away on a plastic mouse while staring into a flickering computer screen. So for the time being at least the brave new world of archaeological publishing needs to embrace both the innovatory and the traditional by developing schemes that build on the progress already made by the revolution in electronic information transfer technologies, while perpetuating a means by which those without computers, or the will to use them, can still get at archaeological results.

At Cotswold Archaeology we currently see three strands to our archaeological publishing programme. For certain kinds of sites and projects the substantial monograph or a report in an appropriate journal remains the objective. The publication of the final reports on the Cirencester Excavation programme of the 1960s through to the 1990s are examples of such works, although in future we imagine that the printed texts will be supplemented by additional material posted on the internet to provide, for example, access to the archives, databases, and more photographs and pictures than can be included in a conventional publication. At the opposite end of the spectrum we will continue to produce in-house client reports together with short summary accounts of all the projects we undertake for listing in our own *Annual Report*, for inclusion in the annually produced *Gazetteer of Archaeological Investigations in England*, and for selective use in other suitable places. These summaries provide up-to-date guides to what is happening and what has been found; they are indispensable tools for contracting archaeologists and researchers alike to keep abreast of new work and to track down copies of client reports and related material. Many of these indexes and gazetteers are being migrated into new formats in order to provide on-line access, and we welcome this.

Between these extremes is a third strand which involves the production of printed reports that are widely distributed free of charge. Two channels are being developed to promote this innovatory approach. Projects outside Gloucestershire and the Bristol area will be published through a series of Cotswold Archaeology Occasional Papers. One has already been produced (as it happens relating to work inside Gloucestershire) and copies have been deposited in local libraries and public institutions, all university libraries in the UK that serve an established archaeology department, the national copyright libraries, and the libraries of the appropriate national museums, sites and monuments records, and national and regional amenity societies. Interested individuals can purchase printed copies or down-load a version from our internet site. Important projects that relate to Gloucestershire and the Bristol region will be included in an occasional series of numbered supplements issued alongside the *Transactions of the Bristol and Gloucestershire Archaeological Society*. We have christened these supplements our **Bristol and Gloucestershire Archaeological Reports**. This volume is the first such report, and we would welcome comments that might help us improve the usefulness and appeal of future volumes. Distributed free to all personal and institutional members of the Bristol and Gloucestershire Archaeological Society, the reports have been designed so that they are archaeological companions to, and can be shelved and stored alongside, the annual volumes of *Transactions*. Such is the quantity of material now being produced for publication that in some years there will be reports from Cotswold Archaeology in the main body of the *Transactions* as well as in a report supplement.

It may seem like the revival of 19th-century liberalism, but we firmly believe in exchanging as much quality information as possible, as freely as possible, and to as wide an audience as possible. In addition to the *CA Occasional Papers* and *BAGAR* reports there is more information about recent projects on Cotswold Archaeology's web site at *www.cotswoldarch.org.uk*. We sincerely hope that you will find these various pathways for the publication of information acceptable and useful, and that those who pay for archaeological investigations will feel that their contribution to the development of a collective understanding of the past is in one way or another appropriately placed in the public domain.

Professor Timothy Darvill
Chairman of the Board of Directors of Cotswold Archaeology
October 2002

CONTENTS

Foreword iii

Publishing Archaeology: The Cotswold Archaeology Approach iii

Contents 1

Abstract 2

Acknowledgements 2

Introduction 3

Excavation Results 5

The Finds 22

The Biological Evidence 41

Discussion 68

Bibliography 75

ABSTRACT

Excavations at Stoke Road, Bishop's Cleeve in 1997 revealed Romano-British agricultural enclosures, evidence of small-scale ironworking, possible structures and a small burial plot, dating from the 3rd century AD to the last quarter of the 4th century AD. A small post-built structure, probably a temporary shelter or windbreak, was dated by a single sherd of grass-tempered pottery to the Saxon period between the 7th and 9th centuries AD. Medieval remains, dating from the 12th to 15th century, comprised a possible stock enclosure, garden plots and the rear of toft boundaries running perpendicular to the Stoke Road frontage. A small building, with an internal cobbled surface and an external stone-lined drain, and several waterlogged pits were revealed within one toft. The absence of biological remains from other medieval rural sites in Gloucestershire to date makes those from the waterlogged pits of particular note. Evidence of small-scale ironworking from the medieval period was also recovered.

ACKNOWLEDGEMENTS

The writers are grateful to J.J.H. Homes Ltd, which commissioned and funded the excavation and publication of the work, and especially to Peter Allen and Paul Wood for their help and interest. The work was monitored by Jan Wills of Gloucestershire County Council, whose support was greatly appreciated. Thanks also goes to the excavators who worked in difficult weather conditions. We are grateful to all the contributors who have assisted in the preparation of this report and to Dr Keith Wilkinson who integrated and edited the environmental evidence. Neil Holbrook, Niall Oakey and David Aldred kindly commented upon earlier drafts of this text. Charles Parry of Gloucestershire County Council kindly provided information on nearby excavations. Dr Jane Timby would like to thank Dr Alan Vince for his invaluable assistance in identifying the medieval fabrics and for his discussions on the dating and significance of the assemblage.

The project was managed by Dawn Enright and directed in the field by Brona Langton, assisted by Mark Brett. The illustrations are by Richard Morton and Peter Moore. The conservation of selected items was undertaken at the Institute of Archaeology, Oxford. The finds and archive will be deposited with Cheltenham Art Gallery and Museum under Accession Number 1998.9.

INTRODUCTION

In 1997, Cotswold Archaeological Trust (CAT; now Cotswold Archaeology) excavated a 7125m^2 area at Stoke Road, Bishop's Cleeve (NGR: SO 9555 2765). This work, which was in advance of residential development, followed desk-based assessment and field evaluation. The desk-based assessment indicated that the site was located in close proximity to known Romano-British settlement remains, revealed in excavations at nearby Gilders Paddock (Parry 1999) and Home Farm (Hart 1992; Barber and Walker 1998). As the site lay on the periphery of the Saxon and medieval village, it was thought that deposits related to these periods also might extend into the development area (Barber 1996). The archaeological and historical development of Bishop's Cleeve has been reviewed recently (Parry 1999) and therefore will not be repeated here. The site-specific history indicated that it probably lay within the estate of Bishop's Cleeve held by the Bishop of Worcester. The earliest known surviving cartographic evidence is the 1839 Apportionment Map which shows the site to have been in agricultural use. Map evidence indicates that this continued until at least 1954, sometime after which the site became the ground of the local football team.

The field evaluation trenches excavated by CAT revealed archaeological remains dating to both the Roman and medieval periods across the central and southern parts of the development site; elsewhere the presence of deep ponds and former quarry pits appeared to have removed any archaeological remains that may have existed towards the northern end of the site (Fig. 1). Consequently an open area excavation was carried out across the southernmost two-thirds of the site as a condition of the planning consent granted by Tewkesbury Borough Council, and to a brief prepared on their behalf by Gloucestershire County Council Archaeology Service.

Location and geology

The area of excavation lies on the north side of Stoke Road and to the west of Pullar Court, and was part of the former pitch of the Bishop's Cleeve Football Club (Fig. 1). The land lies at approximately 52m AOD, artificially levelled for the pitch. At the southern end of the site the natural topography slopes gently down towards Stoke Road.

The British Geological Survey (BGS) maps the site as lying within an eroded remnant of Cheltenham Sand (BGS 1:50,000 Solid and Drift geology map 217), however at the extreme southern end of the site an area of Lower Lias clay (which underlies the Cheltenham Sand) was apparent. The interface between these strata was observed during archaeological monitoring of several house foundation trenches adjacent to Stoke Road.

Methodology

Topsoil and subsoil were removed under archaeological supervision by mechanical excavator using a toothless grading bucket. Selected areas were hand-cleaned prior to detailed investigation of specific features, concentrating on recovering the plan and structural sequence of the site. Discrete features (such as pits and postholes) were half-sectioned and all linear features (such as ditches) were sectioned once by hand as a minimum (Fig. 2). Certain types of feature, such as burials and structural remains, were fully excavated. A full written, drawn, and photographic record was made, and construction groundworks were monitored subsequently in the area of Lower Lias.

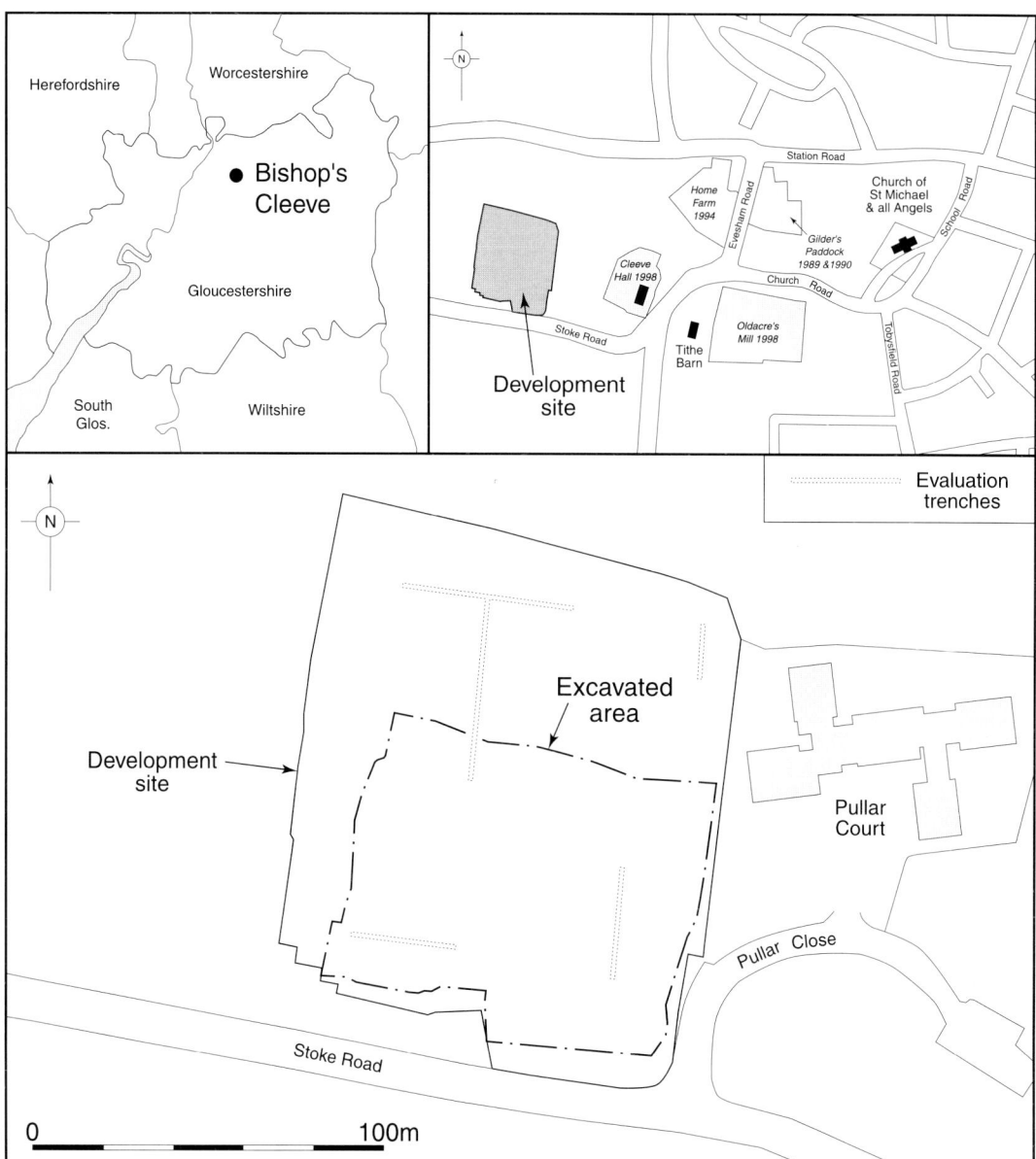

Fig. 1: Location of the site and other excavations at Bishop's Cleeve

EXCAVATION RESULTS

Five periods of activity were identified through stratigraphic relationships and a consideration of the dating evidence:

Period 1: Prehistoric
Period 2: Roman (3rd to 4th century AD)
Period 3: Saxon (7th to 9th century AD)
Period 4 Medieval (12th to 15th century AD)
Period 5 Post-medieval and modern

Features dating to the Roman period were found in the eastern and north-eastern parts of the excavation area, and medieval and later features were concentrated across the southern and western areas, with little overlap between the two. The prehistoric period was represented by residual flintwork only, and Saxon remains were mostly limited to a single structure.

Period 1: Prehistoric

Seven residual flints were recovered of which one, a blade fragment, may be of Mesolithic date. The remainder of the assemblage may be regarded as Late Neolithic/Early Bronze Age. This small assemblage is typical of the local area, and does not provide evidence of actual occupation.

Period 2: Roman (3rd to 4th century AD) (Figs 3 and 4)

Evidence for Romano-British activity comprised two principal elements. In the north-eastern corner of the excavation area a series of ditches (mostly aligned north-west/south-east) formed enclosures and field systems, while to the south lay the remains of pits, gullies (mostly aligned north/south), possible structural evidence and a small burial area. These features represent a number of phases of activity.

Phase 1 comprised a single ditch, 707, which on average was 2m wide and 0.7m deep, and appeared to define the south-western corner of a field, most of which lay beyond the excavation area. Finds recovered from its secondary fill (708) included 3rd to 4th-century potsherds, some cow and horse bone, fragments of hearth lining and a complete smithing hearth-bottom, suggesting a deliberate episode of backfilling. Phase 2 saw the replacement of ditch 707 by ditch 603 (Fig. 10, section 1), which with its south-eastern continuation ditch 628 formed a broadly rectangular enclosure measuring approximately 15m by at least 35m, also extending beyond the limit of excavation. These enclosure ditches were approximately 1.5m wide, up to 0.7m deep and again yielded 3rd to 4th-century potsherds. A single sherd of Midlands shelly ware from its uppermost fill indicates that ditch 628 was still accumulating material into the later 4th century AD. A small quantity of ironworking slag and a few fragments of sheep/goat bone were also recovered from ditch 603. Two features were identified within the enclosure: a small right-angled gully (831) adjacent to ditch 628, and a pit (621) that contained the partial remains of two sheep skeletons. The latter, which was undated, also lay within (and may have been contemporary with) the earlier field defined by ditch 707 (Fig. 10, section 2).

To the south of enclosure 603, the earliest feature appeared to be phase 1 ditch 616 (Fig. 10, section 5), which was aligned north/south and yielded pottery dating to the late 3rd century (Fig. 4). To the north-west of ditch 616 was a shallow gully (833), which produced late 3rd to 4th-

BRISTOL AND GLOUCESTERSHIRE ARCHAEOLOGICAL REPORT NO. 1

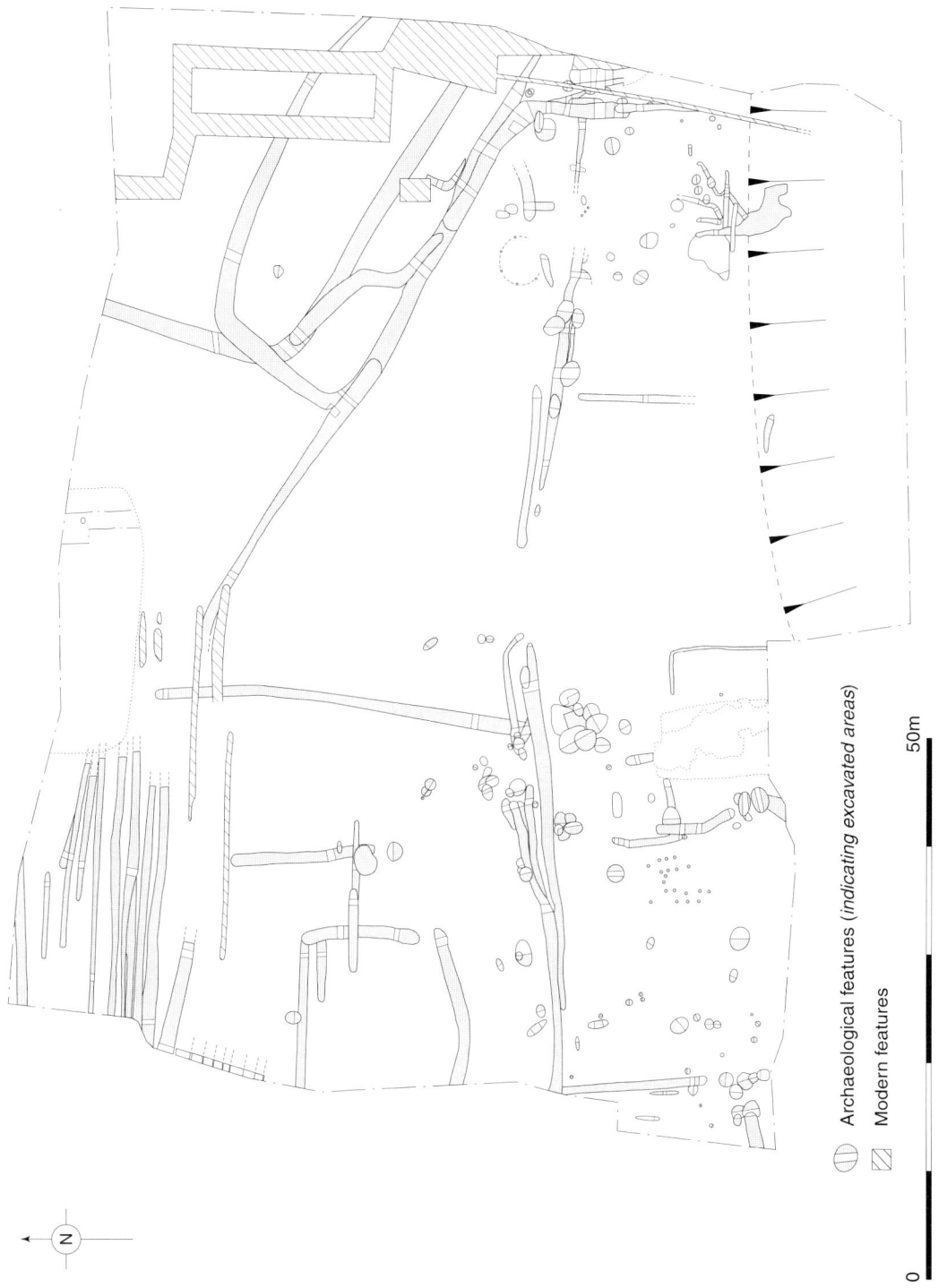

Fig. 2: Plan of all archaeological features, with excavated areas (scale 1:625)

century potsherds. Although heavily truncated by later features, ditch 616 and gully 833 appeared to form the earliest definition of a north/south-aligned boundary that persisted in various forms to the end of the Roman period.

To the west of this north/south boundary, phase 1 land-use was as a small burial plot. Although the area had been subject to later disturbance from ditch-cutting and ploughing (probably from all periods), two burials (and probably a third) were identified and fully excavated. Burial A lay within a north/south grave (641) measuring 1.22m by 0.6m, which survived to a depth of just 0.1m (Figs 3 and 5). It contained the remains of a juvenile (642), with the skull to the south. The short length of the grave suggested that the lower legs may have been bent back or flexed, although most of the lower leg and feet bones were missing. Four limestone blocks on the western edge of the grave may have been the remains of an internal lining; a further limestone block overlay the skull. Fragments of slag and two sherds of 3rd to 4th-century pottery were recovered from the grave fill along with a later intrusive nail.

Burial B, located some 3m to the south of Burial A, also lay within a north/south-aligned grave (644) measuring at least 1.8m by 0.7m (Fig. 5). This grave also survived to a depth of only 0.1m. It contained the skeleton of an adult male (645) in an extended supine position with the skull to the north, part of which had been removed by later ditch 649. The leg bones displayed signs of plough damage. Two iron nails, recovered from the grave fill but not of Roman type, appear to be intrusive. Other finds included a single fragment of ironworking waste and three sherds of 3rd to 4th-century pottery. Fragments of human bone were also recovered from the fill (650) of ditch 649, but these were identified as from an adult female, and thus represent the disturbed remains of another, unidentified, burial.

Burial C was another north/south-aligned grave (785) located 3.5m south-east of Burial B. It measured 1.5m by 0.6m and survived to a depth of 0.14m. Grave 785 had been damaged across its centre by later gully 635, and along its western edge by a modern drain, however, the fragmentary remains of a mature adult male were retrieved from its fill (786). Further fragments of human bone, probably from the same burial, were recovered from the fill (784) of ditch 635. The small size of the burial area suggests it may have been a family plot. Disturbance from subsequent Romano-British ditches may indicate that it went out of use fairly rapidly.

To the east of the burial area, phase 2 saw the redefinition of the north/south boundary by an alignment of four pits (791, 797, 814, 825), all of which produced quantities of iron slag and potsherds dating to the 3rd to 4th centuries. To the south, and on the same alignment, a fifth pit, 827, was identified, but it yielded no pottery or evidence of ironworking waste. Immediately to the east of the pit alignment, ditch 616 was widened and redefined as ditch 799 (Fig. 10, section 5), the fill of which (618) contained late 3rd to 4th-century pottery and a large quantity of ironworking debris including six complete hearth bottoms, again suggesting deliberate backfilling. Ditches 616 and 799 were sealed by a layer (617) also dating to the late 3rd or 4th century and from which five complete hearth bottoms and fragments of hearth lining were recovered. Layer 617 was overlain by layer 745, which produced yet more ironworking debris (see p36). Immediately to the west of the pit alignment, the relationship between a short, shallow, north/south-aligned gully (787) and a longer, shallow, east/west-aligned gully (635) had been lost to later truncation, but both also produced late 3rd to 4th-century pottery and quantities of iron slag including further complete hearth bottoms and fragments of hearth lining. To the north, ditch 649 (cutting across burial B) appeared to be contemporary.

Although the purpose of these features is unclear, it is evident that there was a Romano-British ironworking area nearby, presumably just to the east of ditch 799 beyond the limit of

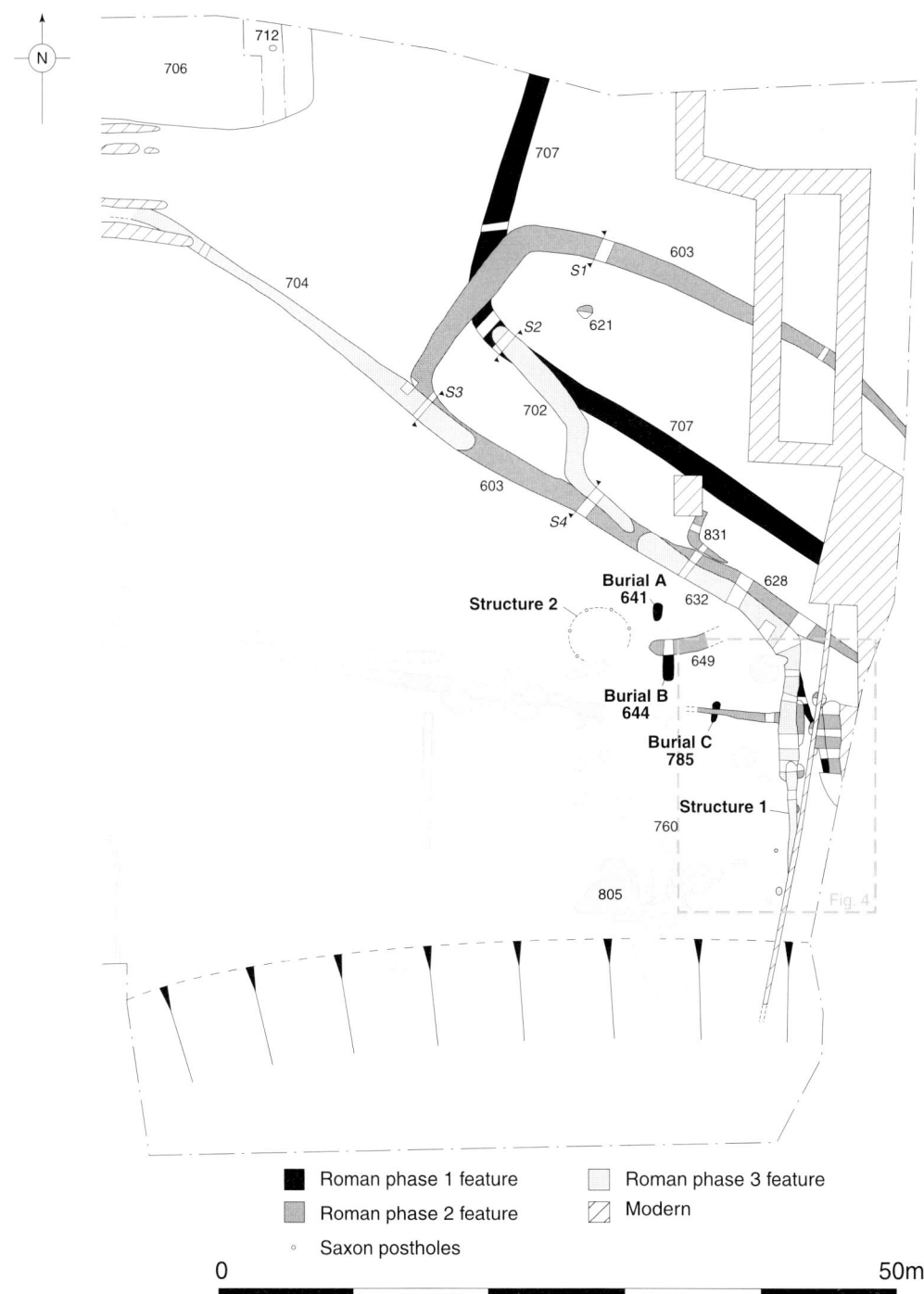

Fig. 3: Phased plan of Roman and Saxon features (scale 1:500)

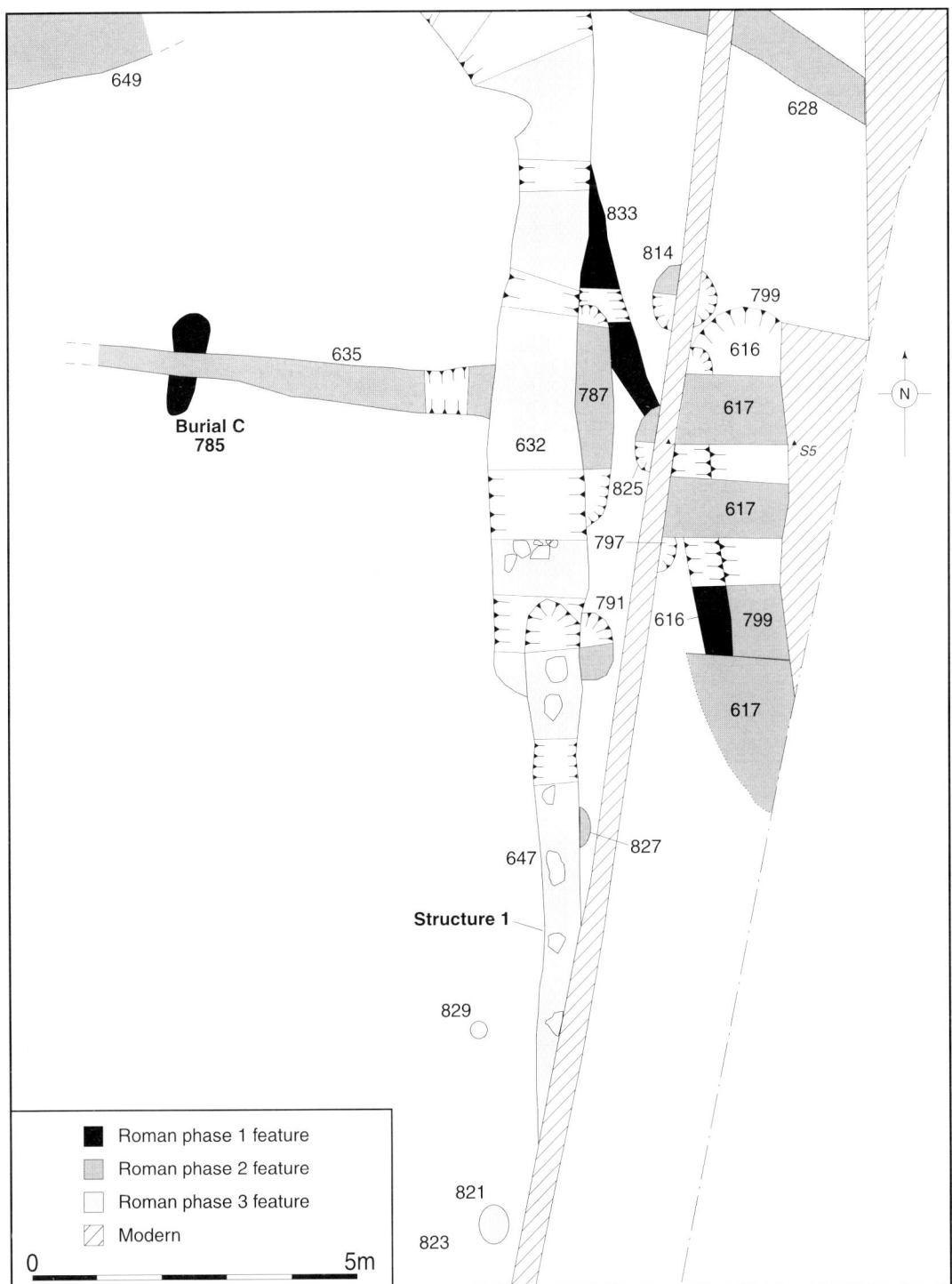

Fig. 4: *Detailed phased plan of Roman features in the vicinity of Structure 1 (scale 1:100)*

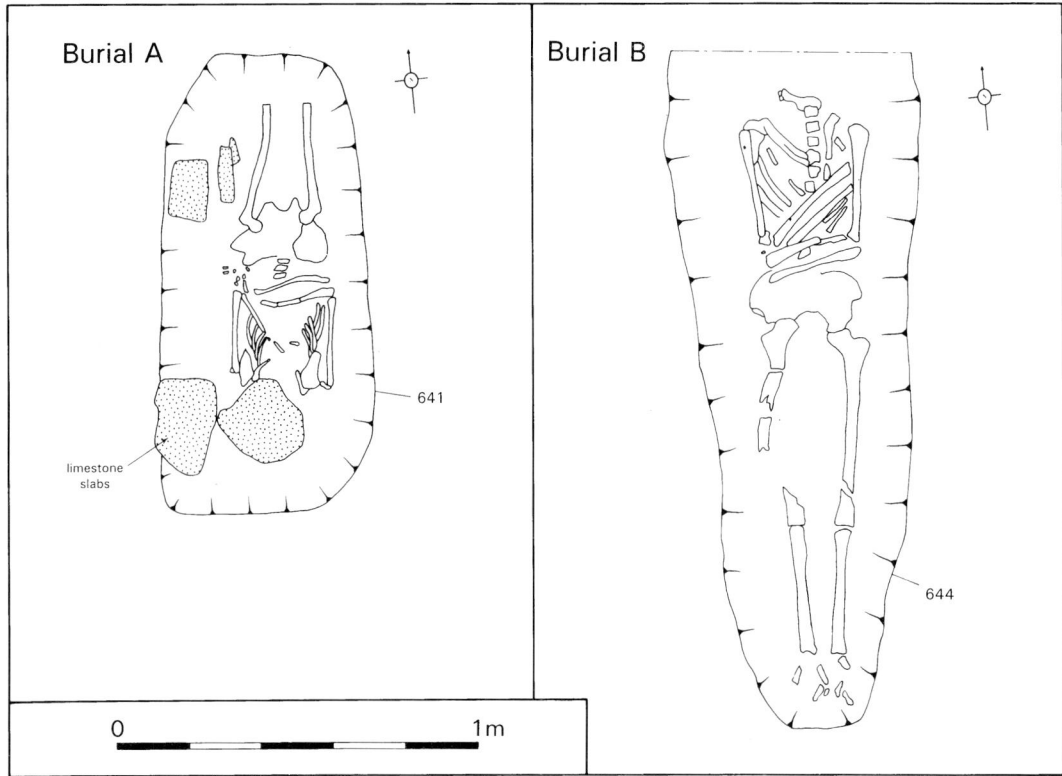

Fig. 5:   Detail of burials A and B (scale 1:20)

excavation. It is possible that the pits and ditch 799 were directly related to the ironworking activity of phase 2, with gullies 787 and 635 perhaps originally acting as drains before all were backfilled with metalworking debris.

The north/south boundary was again redefined during phase 3 with the cutting of ditch 632 (Fig. 10, section 4) through gullies 787, 635 and pit 791. Ditch 632 continued northwards and then turned north-westwards, re-cutting enclosure ditch 603/628 for a distance of approximately 13m. Its upper fill (847) yielded more 3rd to 4th-century pottery, including a single sherd of Midlands shelly ware dating to the later 4th century. Four coins dated to AD 330– 340, probably representing a small hoard, were also recovered from the surface of ditch fill 847.

Other enclosure modifications were recorded that were probably contemporary with ditch 632. Continuing on the alignment of ditch 632 (and probably once contiguous with it), ditch 702 turned north and then north-west again on the alignment of ditch 707, stopping just short of the enclosure's north-western limit. The sherd of medieval pottery recovered with 3rd to 4th-century potsherds from the fill (703) of this ditch must be considered intrusive. Although undated, the position and alignment of ditch 704 (Fig. 10, section 3), extending north-west from the western corner of the enclosure, might also be considered contemporary. It is not clear however whether ditches 632, 702 and 704 replaced the enclosure, or whether they represent redefinitions, internal divisions and extensions of the enclosure.

The last activity of phase 3 was the building of Structure 1. Trench slot 647, which continued the alignment of ditch 632 southwards, was infilled with a compact sand silt 648 (yielding 3rd to

4th-century pottery) and had flat limestone blocks laid in its surface at regular 1m intervals (Fig. 4). The northernmost block had a central rectangular hole, probably to take a tenon of a wooden post, indicating that these were post-pads for a structure (Structure 1). No further evidence of this structure was revealed, and it may be that the rest of it lay beyond the edge of excavation to the east, although evidence may have been lost through ploughing and modern disturbance. Alternatively, the structure may have been a substantial fence, perhaps acting as a windbreak for the iron-smithing area to the east. Postholes 821 and 829 may have been part of this structure, although neither contained any dating evidence and could as easily relate to medieval activity, which included the adjacent posthole 823.

To the south-west of Structure 1, 3rd to 4th-century potsherds and fragments of a Roman quern or millstone were recovered from a stony layer (726) lying within an irregular, shallow medieval feature (805, see below).

Dating evidence

Other than a few sherds of residual 2nd-century pottery, the vast majority of the Roman assemblage dated to the 3rd and 4th centuries AD. There were clearly several stratigraphic phases of Roman-British activity, however, these phases were not apparent within the pottery assemblage other than in the presence of late 4th-century Midlands shelly ware from the upper fills of some of the ditches. A mid 4th-century presence is also apparent from the coin hoard from the top of ditch 632.

Period 3: Saxon (7th to 9th century) (Fig. 3)

Evidence of Saxon activity was extremely limited. Five postholes, located to the west of the Romano-British burials, enclosed an area approximately 4m in diameter, and formed two-thirds of a circular structure (Structure 2). Despite careful cleaning no traces of further postholes were identified. The small scale of Structure 2 suggests a temporary shelter or windbreak. A single sherd of pottery which can be broadly dated to the Saxon period was retrieved from the fill (742) of a Structure 2 posthole.

A single sherd of Saxon pottery was also recovered from isolated posthole 712 at northern edge of the excavation area. The posthole was overlain by a later medieval layer (706), from which two further sherds of residual Saxon pottery were recovered, one suggestive of a broad 7th to 9th-century AD date. In addition, a residual 9th-century copper alloy strap-end, decorated with a zoomorphic motif (Fig. 16.2), was recovered from pit 760 (dated to 12th to 14th century).

Period 4: Medieval (12th to 15th century) (Figs 6, 7, 8 and 9)

Evidence of medieval activity included ditches, pits, the remains of a barn or stable, and a possible drain. Associated pottery suggests that this activity dates to the 12th to 14th centuries. The medieval remains were subdivided by boundary ditches into four plots (A to D) in the southern half of the excavation area, and three enclosures (E to G) to the west (Fig. 6). There was very little overlap between the medieval and Romano-British remains due to a possible medieval field (H) in the north-eastern quarter of the site.

At the southern end of plots C and D, the ground sloped down to the south towards Stoke Road forming a distinct depression. As a medieval drain ran down this slope, the inference is that the slope existed at that time. The depression is therefore thought to represent a medieval pond or perhaps hollow, possibly formed as a result of stream action. Deposits within the depression

Fig. 6: Plan of all medieval features, and locations of plots and enclosures (scale 1:625)

were not excavated archaeologically, but were subject to sampling with monolith tins during subsequent archaeological monitoring of the construction of three houses (see p67).

The boundary ditches (Fig. 6)

A series of ditches and gullies, intermittently cut by pits, was found across the southern part of the site. They appear to have defined the rear limits of medieval tofts that fronted onto Stoke Road to the south. The ditches were predominantly aligned east/west, and occurred in two groups: ditches 672 and 658 to the east, and ditches 837, 964 and 980 to the west. A gap of 9m between the two probably provided access to field H to the north.

Of the western group (Fig. 7), ditch 837 survived for a length of 34m. Towards its eastern end, at its intersection with ditch 810, it cut ditch 986, and was in turn cut by pits 842 and 848. To the north of ditch 837, ditches 858 and 964 ran parallel. Ditch 858 was cut by a series of pits (896, 892 and 913), while ditch 964, which survived for a length of 10m, was cut by ditch 980. The latter was the latest in the group and was itself cut by pit 1045. The majority of these features contained small quantities of animal bone in their fills, but no ironworking debris was recovered.

Of the eastern group (Fig. 8), ditch 672 survived for a length of 15m. Although no dating evidence was recovered, other finds retrieved from its fill (673) included a smithing hearth bottom. Ditch 658 ran parallel to 672 and continued eastwards for a further 10m, where gully 670 ran parallel. Gully 670 had been truncated at both ends: to the west by pit 777, from which slag debris and 12th to 14th-century pottery was recovered, and to the east by pit 692, which, along with pits 688 and 654, also cut through ditch 658. Pits 780, 688 and 654 contained small quantities of animal bone and, in the case of pit 688, ironworking debris.

The alignment appears to have continued to the eastern limit of the excavation, through ditch 774 to intercutting pits 611 and 619 (Fig. 11, section 9). Pit 611 yielded both Roman and medieval potsherds as well as more metalworking debris, and was sampled for palaeoenvironmental analysis (see p49).

The area to the south of the east/west-aligned ditches was divided by three north/south alignments of ditches and pits into four enclosures or plots (A to D).

Plot A (Fig. 7)

Plot A was only partially exposed during excavation. It was divided from plot B by ditch 1007, which yielded a small quantity of 12th to 14th-century pottery from its fill (1008). The ditch was 17m long and terminated to the south leaving a 1m-wide access, beyond which the boundary continued as a series of intercutting pits (1161, 1165, 1163, 1155 and 1159). The pits were all fairly similar in size, depth and fill.

Although only a small part of plot A was excavated, a number of internal features were identified. Of these, three intercutting shallow pits (1151, 1157 and 1153) contained small quantities of 12th to 14th-century pottery. Ditch 1149, which may have been a sub-division of the plot, yielded a single iron nail and 12th to 14th-century pottery, and gully 1029 yielded 12th to 13th-century pottery. None of the other features yielded datable finds, and no evidence of economic activity was recovered.

Plot B (Fig. 7)

Plot B was 22m wide and at least 22m long. It was divided from plot A by ditch 1007 and from plot C by three short ditches (1105, 1097 and 1195) and a group of intercutting pits (1197, 1199, 1201 and 1203). A 3m-wide gap in this boundary, perhaps representing access between plots B

Fig. 7: Detail of plots A, B and the western part of plot C (scale 1:250)

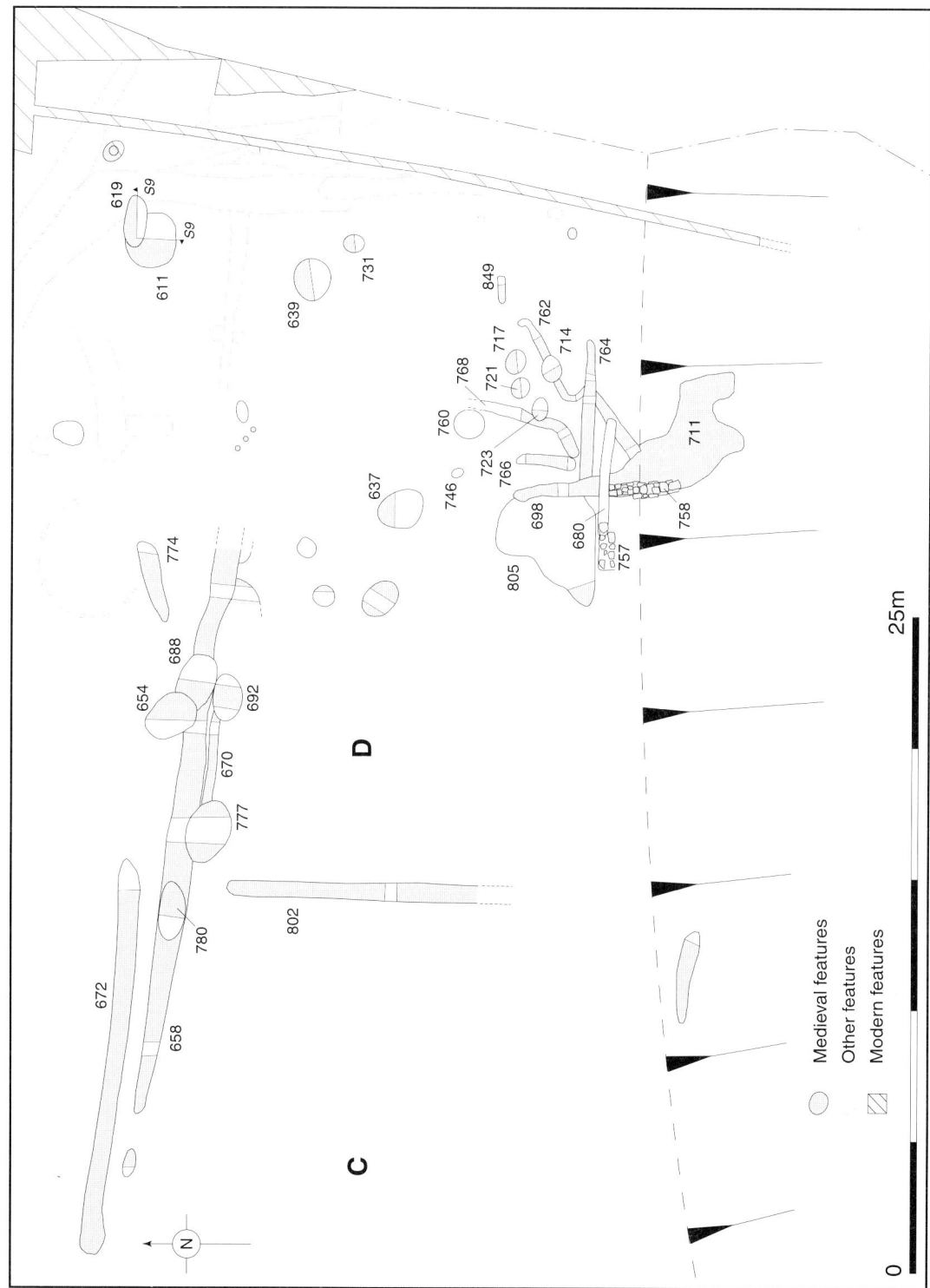

Fig. 8: Detail of the eastern half of plot C, and plot D (1:250)

and C, separated the northern end of ditch 1105 from a group of intercutting pits (including pit 1064) located adjacent to the common northern boundary ditch 837.

Within the plot a number of pits (e.g. pit 1019) and postholes dating to the 12th to 14th century were identified. The primary function of the pits remained undetermined: although a few contained small quantities of domestic refuse, there was not enough to suggest rubbish disposal as their original purpose. Two fills (1021, 1024) from pit 1019 were sampled for palaeoenvironmental analysis (see p49). The postholes were located within the eastern half of the plot, six of which formed a very small rectangular structure (Structure 3), measuring 1m by 1.5m. No dating evidence or function was apparent, but such a small structure may have been used to house domestic fowl.

Plot C (Figs 6, 7 & 8)
Plot C was 40m wide and at least 22m long. Its northern boundary was defined by the east/west-aligned ditches and contained a 9m-wide gap leading to field H. The eastern half of the plot was devoid of evidence of activity, with cut features almost entirely concentrated to the west. The south-eastern corner of the plot sloped down to the depression described above.

The earliest deposits identified within plot C were silty sands (including 1194), which included fragments of animal bone and 12th to 14th-century pottery and were interpreted as trampled layers. These had been cut through by three pits including circular pit 1184, the primary fill (1183) of which contained charred plant remains (Fig. 7; see p49). The secondary fill 1182 was highly compact, which suggested the pit had been deliberately backfilled. All three pits were sealed by a series of dumped layers, including layer 1130 containing fragments of Roman brick and tile together with glazed medieval roof tile and 12th to 14th-century pottery. Layer 1130 is interpreted as a levelling layer, deposited deliberately to raise the ground level and form a preparation layer for an irregular cobbled surface (1111), which survived over an area measuring 10.5m by 4.5m (Fig. 9). Just to the west, two more levelling layers (1131, 1185) were recorded underlying layer 1130.

Surface 1111 comprised fragments of limestone with occasional fragments of re-used Roman brick and tile, and also fragments of two medieval rotary querns. The surface was worn in places, suggesting episodes of patching-up or localised areas of heavy use. To the east and cutting through the earlier trampled layers was a stone-lined, 'L'-shaped drain (1109), which ran for almost 4m before turning southwards for 9m and beyond the edge of excavation. It was lined with pegged limestone roof slates, presumably reused from a nearby derelict or demolished medieval building of some status. The slates were set vertically against the edges of the drain, with further slates laid flat across the top to form a cover. At the western end of the drain, fragments of roof slate were set vertically in a circle, suggesting a down-pipe had once been present.

Although no evidence for walls was found, the remains suggest the former presence of a roofed structure (Structure 4), probably a stable or shed, in this part of plot C. The drain was probably external to two sides of structure. There appears to have been an entrance at the northern end of the building, just to the west of the drain terminus, where two large flat stones lying approximately 2.7m apart acted as post-pads. Levelling layer 1130 extended halfway across this entrance, whereas cobbled surface 1111 respected it, suggesting that the entrance may have had a stone threshold. Posthole 1168 was the only other feature surviving internally, although ditch 1125, linking the building with the western boundary of the plot, was also clearly related. The remains of Structure 4 were sealed by layer 1112 (not illustrated), containing pottery dating up to the 15th century, which dates the demolition of this structure.

Fig. 9: Structure 4: the medieval stable or shed (scale 1:100)

To the north of the drain and cobbled surface was a cluster of large intercutting pits (including 1013, 1068 and 1091: Fig. 7) also dating to the 12th to 14th centuries, two of which contained further organic remains. Pit 1091 (Fig. 11, section 8) contained waterlogged plant remains within its basal fill (1092), which were sampled for palaeoenvironmental analysis. Pit 1068 (Fig. 11, section 7), which measured 2.5m by 2m, was of particular note as it contained the remnants of a wattle lining. Its primary fill 1072 was waterlogged and rich in organic material including seeds, fruits, buds, charred crop remains and insect fauna (see p49). Finds retrieved from this fill included two fragments of a leather shoe (see p33). A layer of disturbed natural sand (303, 404, 1113: not illustrated) around the pit cluster was interpreted as the effects of trampling.

To the west of the pits was linear pit 1114, which was filled with rubble and capped with flat stones and roof slate. No function was identified for this feature and no dating evidence was retrieved, but its location within an area of medieval activity and the fact that it ran parallel to the east/west boundary ditches suggests it was contemporary.

Plot D (Fig. 8)

Plot D was a minimum of 26m wide and was divided from plot C by north/south-aligned ditch 802. Ditch 802 petered out just short of the depression that occupied the southern half of plot D. The majority of features recorded in plot D were gullies and pits, many of them intercutting within an area towards the eastern end of the plot, at the top of the southern slope.

The earliest feature appeared to be pit 805. This large, irregular feature, measuring approximately 4m² but only 0.35m deep, may have been a natural hollow infilled by redeposited natural sands (yielding medieval potsherds) and a stony deposit (726) containing only Romano-British pottery and worked stone. Another fill (796) of pit 805 was sampled for palaeoenvironmental evidence (see p49). Immediately adjacent was a shallow layer (806) containing an ashlar block (see p33). Just to the east were two irregular but shallow gullies (762 and 768), which were cut across by an east/west-aligned gully (764), respected by a short north/south-aligned gully (766). All had similar profiles and dimensions, and had similar silt fills from which no dating evidence was recovered. The two earlier gullies may have been drains, the later gullies possibly internal divisions. Gully 764 and pit 805 had later been cut by north/south-aligned gully 698, that at its northern end was merely a narrow channel, but which widened considerably once it reached the slope to the south. Two of its fills (699 and 700) were characteristic of a natural silting-up process, and both contained 12th to 14th-century pottery. The western edge of the gully 698 was revetted with a crude wall (758) of two courses of irregular limestone blocks. A perpendicular alignment of stones (757) to the west of the gully may have been contemporary, but its function was not clear. Gully 698 was probably a drain, channelling water into the depression to the south (see p66). The wider part of the gully had been infilled with a layer of limestone rubble (711), perhaps as an attempt to create a ramp or access across this feature. Layers of silty sand (684, 686) built up over rubble 711 before another east/west-aligned gully (680) was created eastwards of stone alignment 757, perhaps demarcating another internal plot division.

Several pits were recorded within plot D, including 639, 731 and 746, all of which yielded 12th to 14th-century pottery. Pits 637 and 849 also contained ironworking waste, and complete hearth bottoms were recovered from pit 760 along with items of Saxon, medieval and post-medieval metalwork (see p35). A cluster of pits was identified nearby, two of which (714 and 723) contained basal fills characterised by blackened soils overlain by limestone fragments. Although no *in situ* burning was identified these pits appear to contain the remnants of hearth material. Again both contained pottery of 12th to 14th-century date.

Enclosures E, F and G, and field H (Fig. 6)

To the north of the plot B were three enclosures (E, F and G) defined by ditches and occasional pits. Ditch 810 marked the division between these enclosures and field H to the east. It ran perpendicularly to and did not continue beyond ditch 837, indicating that they were broadly contemporary. Enclosure E was located immediately to the north of plot B. The gap east of ditch 964 may have once formed an access between the two, which was subsequently blocked by the cutting of ditch 837 and a cluster of pits, including 975 and 988 (see Fig. 7). Pottery from the 12th to 14th-centuries recovered from these pits indicate their medieval date, but the accompanying fragments of animal bone were not in sufficient quantity to suggest that the primary (or even secondary) use of these pits was for the disposal of rubbish. Further pits recorded to the west of the pit cluster yielded no dating evidence but were presumed also to be medieval in origin.

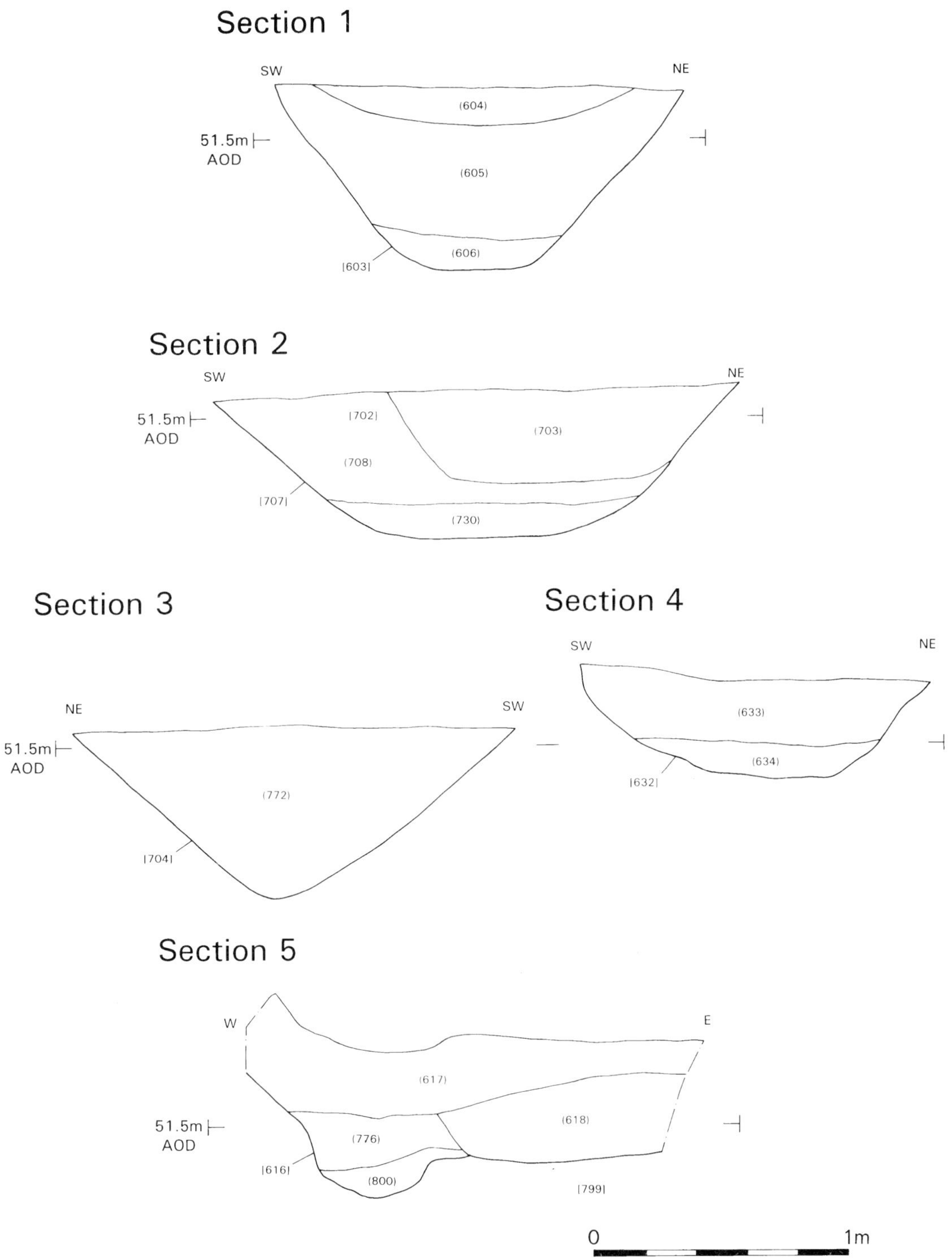

Fig. 10: *Sections through Roman ditches and gullies (scale 1:25)*

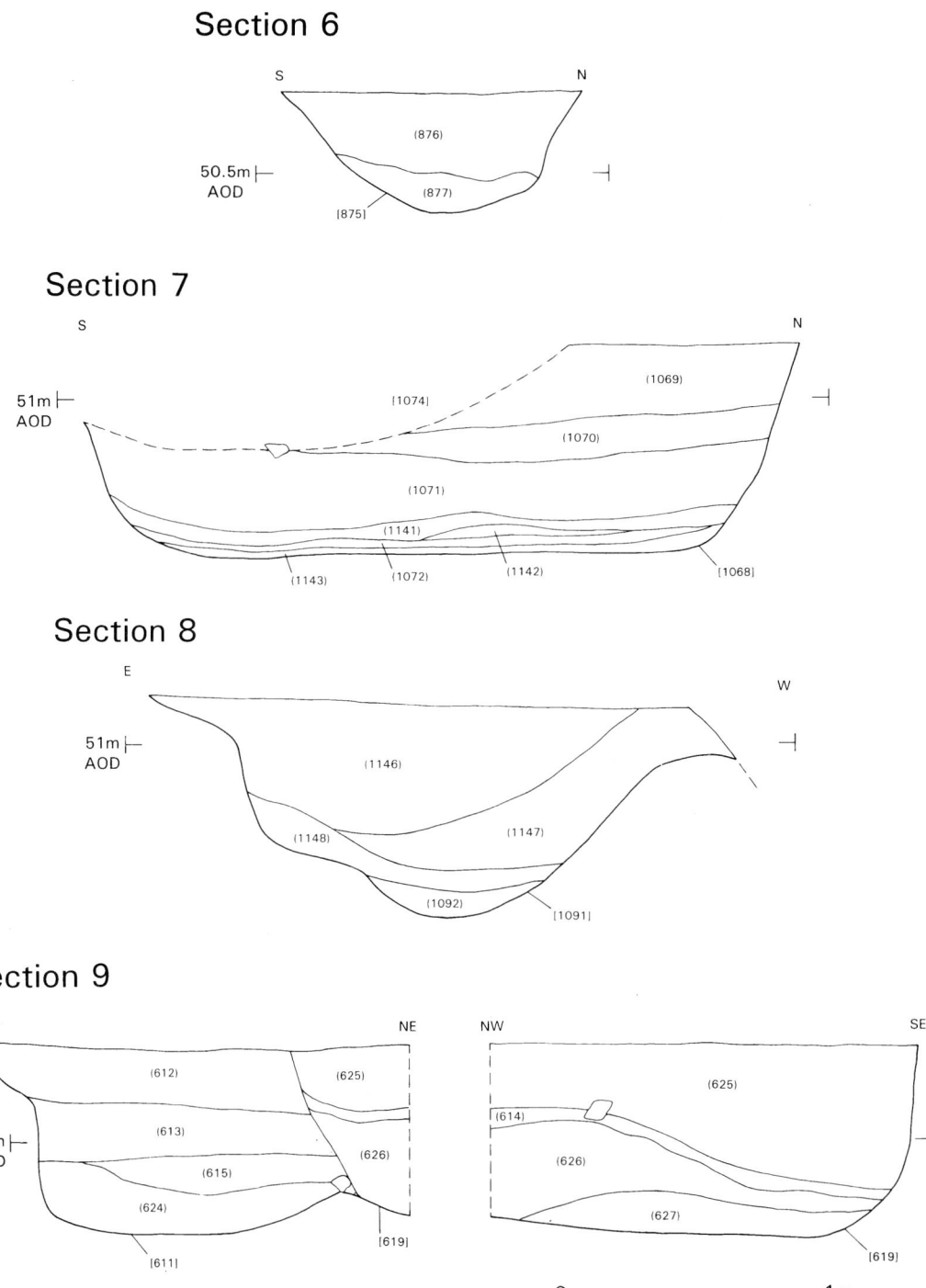

Fig. 11: Sections through medieval gullies and pits (scale 1:25)

Enclosure F was defined by ditches 949, 944 and 901, enclosing an area of at least 195m^2. A gap between the southern end of ditch 944 and the eastern end of ditch 901 formed an access into this enclosure, which may have served as an animal pen. The enclosure was dated to the 12th to 14th century from pottery retrieved from ditch 944. The only internal feature identified was a short section of undated ditch (947). To the north of enclosure E, Enclosure G was defined by ditches 810, 937 and 816. Pottery dating to the 12th to 14th centuries was recovered from some of these ditches. Several pits were also identified, decreasing in density to the north, away from the apparent focus of settlement to the south.

To the north of enclosures F and G, a series of east/west-aligned shallow gullies was probably representative of ploughing, suggestive of an arable field in this vicinity. These included ditches 875 (Fig. 11, section 6), 916 and 934. Pottery of 12th to 14th-century date was recovered from several of these gully fills. Ditch 875 was sampled for palaeoenvironmental study (see p49).

It is the absence of medieval remains from the north-eastern quarter of the site that leads to its interpretation as a field (H). Access was probably from plot C via the gap in the ditches, which was flanked by two small pits (854, 856) on its western side. In contrast to the plough furrows surviving to the west, and from the survival of earlier Romano-British remains, field H appears to have been predominantly medieval pasture. The presence of layer 706 at the northern end of the site, which yielded both medieval and Saxon potsherds, and the medieval potsherds recovered from layer 701/623/756 (not illustrated) overlying the Romano-British burials to the north of plot D, suggest that some fertilisation of the field took place in the medieval period.

Dating evidence

The assemblage of medieval pottery presents a surprisingly tight group chronologically. While a relatively small group of wares could potentially date from the late 12th to mid 13th century, most of the vessels date to the second half of the 13th century extending into the 14th century; moreover, most of the earlier vessels occur alongside slightly later material, suggesting either the use of accumulated midden material to backfill features or certain forms being curated longer. Nearly all of the later wares, continuing into the 15th century, were recovered from surface layers overlying and sealing the negative features.

The pottery assemblage therefore mostly represents one phase of activity dating from the late 12th to the 14th century. While there was clearly some redefinition and/or realignment of features during this time, there was no obvious chronological development of the site during this period. It is only with the 15th-century wares recovered from surface deposits sealing earlier remains that a chronological division is apparent. In effect this dates the abandonment of this part of medieval Bishop's Cleeve.

Period 5: Post-medieval and modern

Post-medieval evidence was confined to occasional stray finds of metalwork, presumably incorporated into earlier ditch fills through continued ploughing in the post-medieval period. Occasional pits were also identified, one of which (920, not illustrated) cut through medieval gullies 916 and 918 (Fig. 6) and contained the remains of a horse and some dog bones within its backfill (921).

The eastern edge of the site was heavily disturbed by modern structures, including the foundations of the former football pavilion. A series of field drains was present across the entire excavation area.

THE FINDS

Struck Flint, by Graeme Walker

Seven pieces of flint, comprising two cores, three flakes and two burnt flints (one of which was worked) were recovered. The worked pieces were struck from gravel pebbles and possibly some imported better quality material. Both thick squat flakes and more controlled longer flakes, including a burnt blade segment, are present, indicating an assemblage of mixed date. The assemblage recovered from the nearby Home Farm excavations included utilised flakes and tools (Barber and Walker 1998, 124), but none of these are present at Stoke Road. The assemblage may be Neolithic/Early Bronze Age in date, although a Mesolithic date may be more appropriate for the blade fragment.

The Pottery, by Jane Timby

The evaluation and subsequent excavation produced 2878 sherds of pottery (31.75kg). The bulk of the assemblage, approximately 85% by count, dates to the medieval period, 15% to the Roman period and just four sherds to the Saxon period. No wares dating after the 15th century were recovered.

The pottery was sorted into fabric types based on macroscopic observation assisted with a x20 binocular microscope. Many of the fabrics can be paralleled with sherds from the Roman and medieval type-series currently housed at Gloucester City Museum, but the Roman codes have been adjusted to conform with the format used for the National Roman fabric series (Tomber and Dore 1998), while the medieval fabrics retain the Gloucester numeric codes (see Vince 1983, 141 for summary list). The sorted fabrics were quantified by sherd count, weight and estimated vessel equivalent for each excavated context and the data summarised on a computer spreadsheet (available in the site archive).

The pottery is discussed by period and a summary description of the relevant fabrics can be found below each section. Most of the wares were in a relatively good state of preservation, the average weight of the Roman sherds being 14g and the medieval slightly lower at 10.5g.

Period 2: Roman (Table 1)

The Roman assemblage comprised 436 sherds, largely dating to the 3rd and 4th centuries AD. Most of the material was recovered from the enclosure ditches on the eastern half of the site. Several of the later medieval pits in this area contained a few residual Roman sherds. The fabric repertoire is limited, with 66% of the group being products of the local Severn Valley industry. Malvernian wares of Roman date were surprisingly rare, accounting for 8.5% by count, less than the longer distance-traded Dorset BB1 which accounts for 10%.

The assemblage is extremely conservative and continental imports are limited to five sherds of samian. Other regional imports include products of the Oxfordshire industry, Midlands grog-tempered storage jar and Midlands late Roman shelly ware. Tablewares are poorly represented, suggesting a fairly low status establishment.

The Midlands shelly ware, although limited to just three sherds, indicates use of the area in the last quarter of the 4th century.

Description of Roman fabrics and forms

IMPORTS
Samian (CG SAM)
Only five sherds of Central Gaulish samian were present, mostly in fairly abraded condition.

LOCAL
Severn Valley wares (SVW OX2) (Webster 1976; Rawes 1982)
Both oxidised and grey wares have been subsumed into this group within which there are a number of minor fabric variations. A single sherd of a limestone-tempered variant was present and several pieces from handmade storage jars (Gloucester TF23). There is a diverse range of forms, mainly jars, bowls and tankards. Rim forms include bifid, hooked, everted and triangular pendant: types current in the 3rd and 4th centuries. An unusual handled bowl from fill 776 of ditch 616 is illustrated (Fig. 12.1).

Malvernian ware (MAL RT)
A brown or black, moderately hard ware containing fragments of Malvernian rock. The handmade variant (Peacock 1967, Group A) was very rare, most of the sherds belonging to the later wheelmade industry. Vessels include flanged bowls and straight-sided dishes in the BB1 tradition and everted rim jars.

Micaceous grey ware (MIC GW)
A generally light-textured, well-fired sandy ware, usually grey or black in colour, occasionally orange-brown. The sandy texture of the fabric varies considerably from moderately coarse to fine, but is always characterised by the prominent presence of fine white mica (muscovite). Sparse dark-grey rounded clay pellets are also usually present. The group undoubtedly contains a number of sub-types but at present it is not possible to make any meaningful distinctions. Although a particularly wide range of forms was made in this fabric, including wheelmade copies of DOR BB1 and SVW OX types, only one featured vessel was present here, a slightly unusual carinated jar (Fig. 12.6).

REGIONAL IMPORTS
Dorset black-burnished ware (DOR BB1) (Williams 1977; Holbrook and Bidwell 1991, 88-138)
Black-burnished ware is the second commonest Roman fabric by count and weight at 10%. Vessels include the most typical 4th-century types, for example conical flanged bowls, well-everted jars with oblique lattice and straight-sided dishes.

Oxfordshire Whitewares (OXF WH) (Young 1977, 93-112)
Featured sherds include a single necked jar (Young type BW2) with blackened exterior surfaces.

Oxfordshire Parchment ware (OXF PA) (Young 1977, 80-92)
Represented by a single bodysherd with red painted decoration.

Oxfordshire Red-slipped wares (OXF RS/OXF RSM) (Young 1977, 123-84)
Vessels include a dish, Young type C45 and mortaria.

Midlands grog-tempered ware (PNK GT) (Booth and Green 1989, 77-84)
Large handmade storage jars dating to the 3rd to 4th century. Represented by just seven bodysherds.

Shell-tempered ware (ROB SH)
A fairly hard, mostly wheelmade ware with a smooth, soapy feel. The paste contains a moderate to common frequency of fossil shell up to 3mm in size and sparse black shale/mudstone. Vessels are usually a pale reddish-brown to dark grey in colour. Although represented by just three bodysherds the ware is a good indicator of continuing activity in the area in the last quarter of the 4th century.

SOURCE UNKNOWN
Local greyware (LOC GW)
A miscellaneous category for various grey, medium sandy wares of unknown provenance.

Catalogue of illustrated Roman sherds (Fig. 12)
1. Handled globular bowl, SWV OX2. Fill 776 of ditch 616.
2. Wide-mouthed jar. SVW OX2. Fill 776 of ditch 616.
3. Plain, straight-sided dish, DOR BB1. Fill 776 of ditch 616.
4. Tankard, SVW OX2. Fill 629 of trench slot 628.

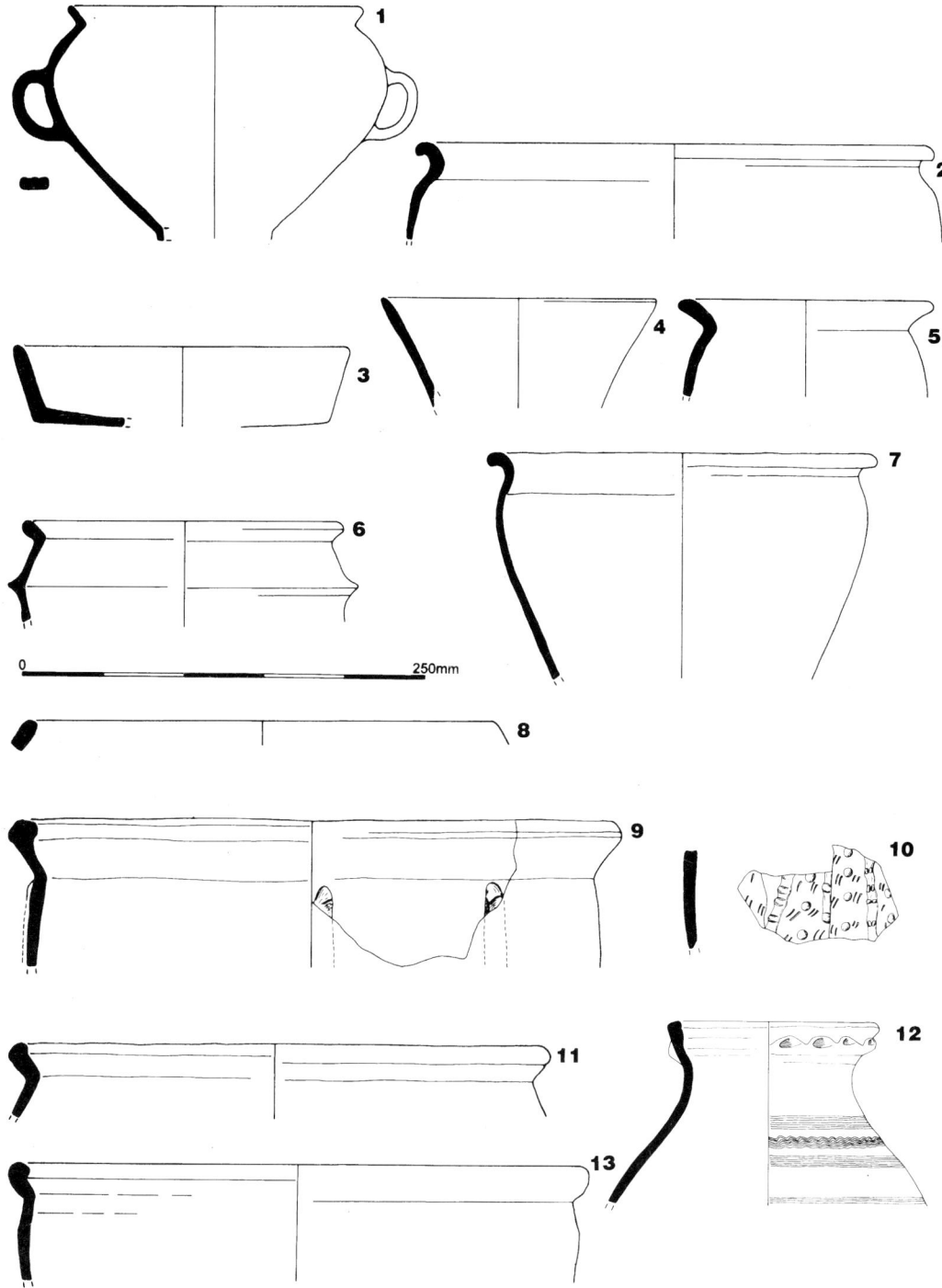

Fig. 12: Roman (nos 1-7) and medieval (nos 8-13) pottery (scale 1:4)

5. Wheelmade, everted rim jar, MAL RT. Light grey, hard, slightly granular fabric with fragments of fine Malvernian rock. Fill 648 of ditch 647.
6. Wheelmade, sharply carinated grey ware jar, MIC GW. Fill 617 of ditch 616.
7. Hard, well-fired grey SVW OX2 necked jar. Fill 617 of ditch 616.

Table 1: Total quantities of Roman fabrics
  : less than 1%; EVE: Estimated Vessel Equivalent

Source	Fabric	Name	No.	%	Wt (g)	%	EVE	%
Local	SVW OX2	Severn Valley Ware	275	63	3658	59	188	53
	SVW OX2	SVW Variant	9	2	133	2	0	0
	SVW OX2	SVW Variant	5	1	285	5	0	0
	MAL RT	Malvernian hm	4	1	15	*	0	0
	MAL RO	Malvernian	37	8.5	366	6	21	6
	MIC GW	Micaceous greyware	19	4.5	107	2	15	4
Unknown	LOC GW	Sandy greyware	8	2	106	2	0	0
Regional	DOR BB1	Dorset BB1	44	10	638	10	89	25
	OXF RS	Oxon red slip	7	1.5	51	1	9	2.5
	OXF PA	Oxon parchment	1	*	4	*	0	0
	OXF WH	Oxon whiteware	6	1	55	1	30	8.5
	OXF RSM	Oxon mortaria	6	1	49	1	1	*
	PNK GT	Grog-tempered	7	1.5	553	9	0	0
	ROB SH	Late shelly ware	3	*	35	*	0	0
Import	SAM	Samian	5	1	90	1.5	0	0
Total			436	100	6145	100	353	100

Period 3: Saxon

The Saxon period is represented by just four bodysherds: two residual sherds from medieval layer 706, one from an underlying posthole 712 and one from posthole 741, part of the evidence for circular Structure 2. The sherd from posthole 712 has a dark brown fabric with a black core containing a sparse scatter of rounded white/clear quartz sand (less than 0.5mm) giving a slightly rough feel, rare sandstone and a sparse frequency of burnt organic material. One of the sherds from layer 706 appears to be of the same fabric. Similar sherds have been noted at Cirencester and Burn Ground, Hampnett, perhaps indicative of a source in the Warwickshire/North Gloucestershire area in the early Saxon period (A. Vince, pers. comm.). The other sherd from 706 has a finely micaceous, smooth paste with no visible sand but commensurately more organic matter and sparse grains of ironstone. It is typical of material from the Severn Valley, for example Frocester, and is probably slightly later in date (7th to 9th century). The sherd from posthole fill 742 has a smooth soapy paste with sparse, rounded limestone or voids and a scatter of fine, rounded, quartz visible at x20 magnification. The sherd is red-brown in colour with a black interior surface.

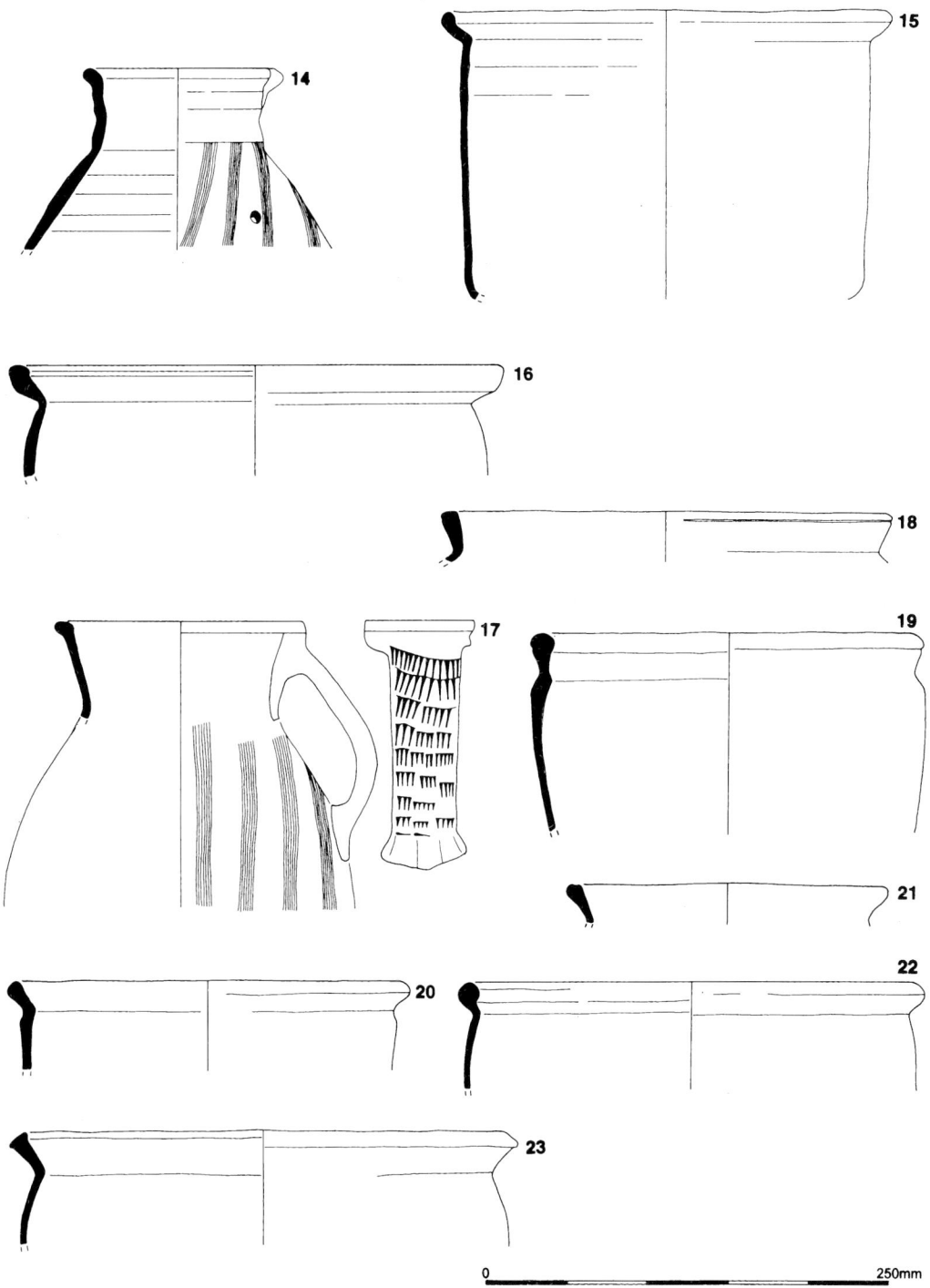

Fig. 13: Medieval pottery (scale 1:4)

Period 4: Medieval (Table 2)

The medieval assemblage comprises some 2400 sherds, most of which appear to date to the second half of the 13th century extending into the 14th century, with a few sherds continuing into the early 15th century. The lower sherd size compared with the Roman assemblage might suggest material that has been subjected to some disturbance. In the absence of any clear stratigraphic divisions the medieval assemblage has been treated as one phase.

Although it is dominated by products of the Malvern Chase industries, accounting for 82% by count, quite a diverse range of other wares is present. Many of these are regionally available tablewares, such as glazed jugs or pitchers from Bristol, Oxfordshire/Buckinghamshire, North Wiltshire and, more locally, Worcestershire. Jars/cooking vessels include wares from Gloucester (TF41B, TF43), the Oxford area (OXY), Hereford (TF42) and Winchcombe.

With the exception of a single sherd of St Neots type (Fig. 12.8) dating to the 10th to 11th century amongst mixed material from layer 706, there is no other recognisable Saxo-Norman pottery present. Among material attributable to the 12th to early 13th century is Gloucester/ Cotswold limestone-tempered ware (TF41B), Herefordshire/Worcestershire sandy ware jars (TF42), Malvernian jars/cooking pots (TF40) and an early glazed Malvernian ware variant, Gloucester TF43 and Winchcombe-type limestone-tempered ware. All of these industries were established by the late 11th century. Jars/cooking pots in TF42 account for 6.5% by count of the total. (At Droitwich TF42 became the principal fabric/form in the 12th to 13th centuries, accounting for nearly half the assemblage there (Hurst 1992, 142).) Other wares that were clearly available at this time were products from the Gloucester area (TF43), Bristol (Ham Green) (TF53) and Minety (TF44).

In the latter part of the 13th to 14th century Malvernian wares dominate, but products from Minety continue to feature. Cotswold limestone-tempered wares had probably been completely displaced by the local TF40 wares. Additional products joining the repertoire at this time are glazed jugs from Worcestershire (TF90) and Oxfordshire/Buckinghamshire (fabric OXAM). (Malvernian wares also appeared more prominently at Droitwich in the 13th to 14th-century assemblages, although Worcester sandy wares still dominate (Hurst 1992, 147).) The latest wares are almost exclusively Malvernian products, including examples of the finer oxidised wares (TF52). Of particular note is a dish with a vertical loop handle. Although traditionally a serving vessel this example has traces of sooting suggesting it has been used for cooking.

Although the medieval assemblage is dominated by jars it does include a significant amount of higher quality tableware in the form of glazed decorated jugs and pitchers. Moreover, these come from a number of local sources. The assemblage therefore reflects a higher status establishment and not peasant households.

Description of medieval fabrics and forms

MALVERNIAN AREA
Malvern Chase ware (TF40)
Characterised by inclusions of granitic Malvernian rock. Vessels range in colour from black, through various shades of grey and brown, to an oxidised orange-brown, the latter being characteristic of the later products. Exclusively found at Bishop's Cleeve as cooking pots, many with sooting on the exterior surfaces. The earliest occurrence of the ware in Gloucester dates to the early 12th century. Earlier vessels are handmade, later vessels have wheel-finished rims, while by the 14th century vessels are generally wheel-thrown. Vessels are generally plain. One unusual example from Bishop's Cleeve has applied thumb-strips (Fig. 12.9). Other examples: Figs 12.11, 13; Figs 13.15, 20, 22, 23; Figs 14.24–27, 31–33.
Early Malvernian type (MAL) (Vince 1977, Group 2)
A sandy ware fabric with occasional fragments of Malvernian rock. Handmade pitchers with a brown external glaze (e.g. Fig. 12.12).

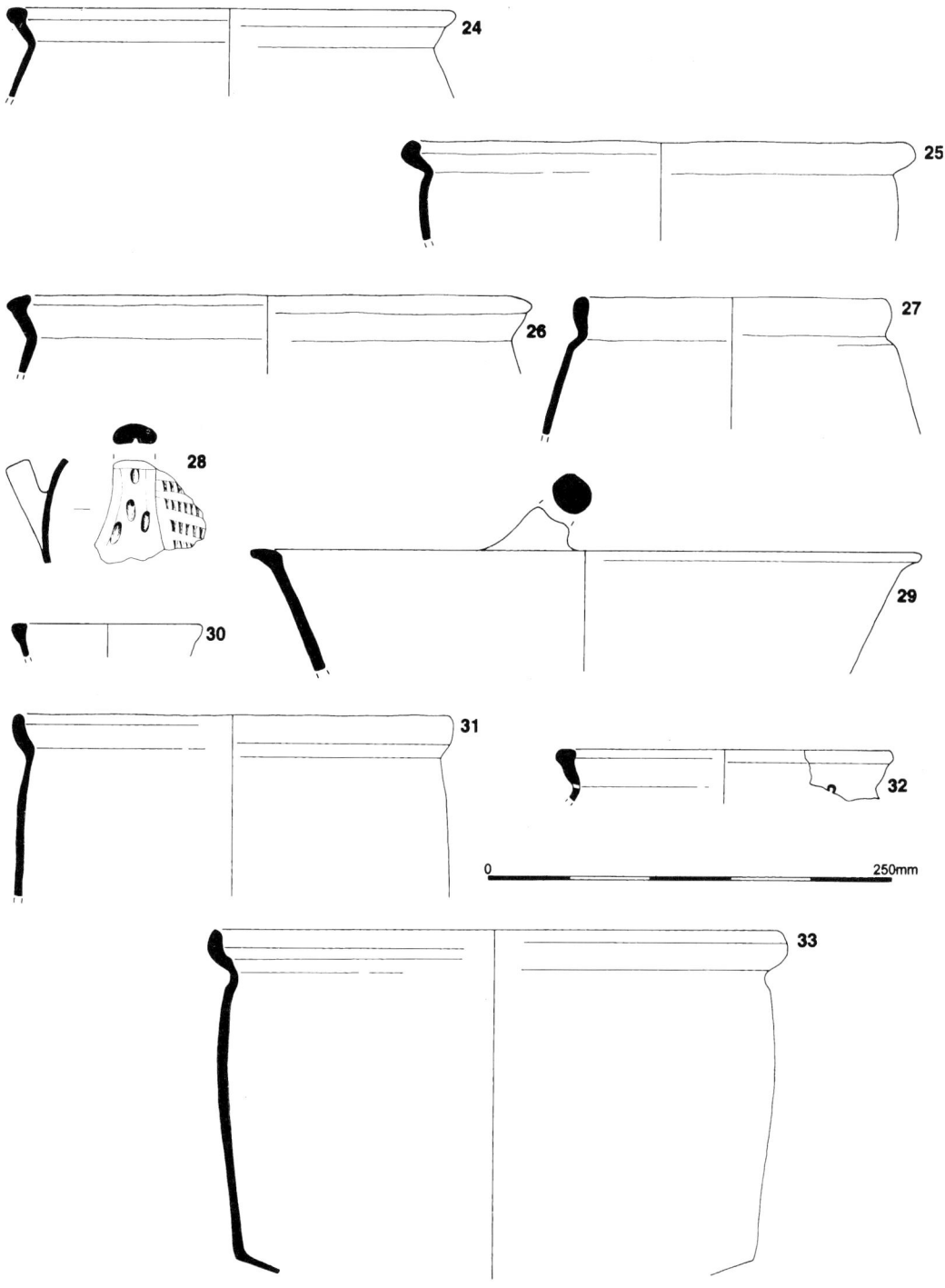

Fig. 14: Medieval pottery (scale 1:4)

Later Malvern Chase ware (TF52)
A finer oxidised ware containing sparse fragments of Malvernian rock. Used for making a variety of wheel-thrown vessels including jugs, jars and dishes (Figs 14.29, 30; Fig. 15.38). First appears in the later 13th–14th centuries. In the 15th, 16th and early 17th centuries, Malvern Chase ware was the most common coarseware in Gloucester. Documentary evidence shows that the industry had ended by 1633 (Vince 1977, 288).

Worcester-type glazed ware (TF90)
Well-fired, grey or orange fabric containing common medium grade quartz sand. Used for making wheel-thrown jugs with green glazed finish. Decoration includes the use of rouletting, floral designs and applied strips and plastic decoration (Fig. 13.17; Fig. 14.28; Fig. 15.39) (=Worcester fabric 64. Hurst and Rees 1992, 207). Current from the mid 13th century.

Herefordshire/Worcester-type unglazed ware (TF42)
Hard, grey medium sandy ware used for generally plain jars. Earlier examples handmade, later wheel-thrown (=Worcester fabric 55, Hurst and Rees 1992, 207), (Figs 13.16, 18).

Winchcombe type (WI) (Vince 1986, 125)
A limestone-tempered ware used for jars. Dated from 10th to 12th century at Winchcombe.

GLOUCESTER AREA

Cotswold oolitic limestone-tempered ware (TF41B)
A mainly reduced, smooth soapy ware containing a moderate to common frequency of oolitic limestone ranging up to 2mm in size.
Mainly used for jars from the mid 11th to early 13th century (Fig. 13.21). Very common in the Gloucester area and probably made locally.

Sand and limestone-tempered ware (TF43)
A hard sandy ware with a scatter of mainly discrete grains of oolitic limestone. Used for handmade jars, often with wheel-finished rims, in the 12th and 13th centuries. One example is decorated with vertical thumbed strips (Fig. 15.35). Petrological analysis has suggested a possible Gloucester source for this ware (Vince 1983, 125).

NORTH WILTSHIRE

Minety-type ware (TF44)
A pale brown ware containing a common to moderate density of fine oolitic limestone often accompanied by grains of iron ore. Occurs as jars and handmade, decorated, spouted pitchers (Fig. 12.10; Fig. 13.14; Figs 15.34, 37). The pitchers and occasionally the jars are completely or partially glazed. Found from 12th to 14th-century contexts in Gloucester.

BRISTOL

Ham Green ware (TF53) (Barton 1963)
Fine sand-tempered fabric with grey clay pellets and occasional limestone. Handmade jugs with a green glaze (e.g. Fig. 15.41). Represented by eight sherds. Late 12th to 13th century.

OXON/BUCKS

St Neots-type ware (Oxford OXR) (Mellor 1994, 54–60)
Smooth, pale brown soapy ware containing fine shell mainly reduced to voids on the surfaces. Represented by a single rimsherd (Fig. 12.8). Very popular in Oxford from the second half of the 10th century, lasting until around the mid 11th century.

Oxon early medieval sandy ware (OXY) (Mellor 1994, 63)
A hard grey or pinkish-orange ware containing abundant sub-angular quartz, occasional rounded clay pellets and polycrystalline quartz. Used for handmade and wheel-thrown vessels including jars (Fig. 15.42) and storage containers. The industry dates from the mid 11th to mid 13th century.

Brill-Boarstall type (OXAM) (Mellor 1994, 111–140).
Hard pale orange/buff ware containing abundant well-sorted quartz sand and frequent fine iron grains. Used for making wheel-thrown vessels, in this case glazed jugs dating from the mid-later 13th to early 15th century.

SOURCE UNKNOWN

Iron-tempered ware (MFE)
A moderately hard, dark brown handmade ware. The paste contains a scatter of distinctive grains of natural iron ore (up to 2mm in size). Occasional fragments of possible igneous rock and grey limestone are also present. An unusual fabric represented by just three featureless sherds and for which no parallel is known. The suggested petrology may indicate a source from the Forest of Dean or Malvernian area. Date uncertain.

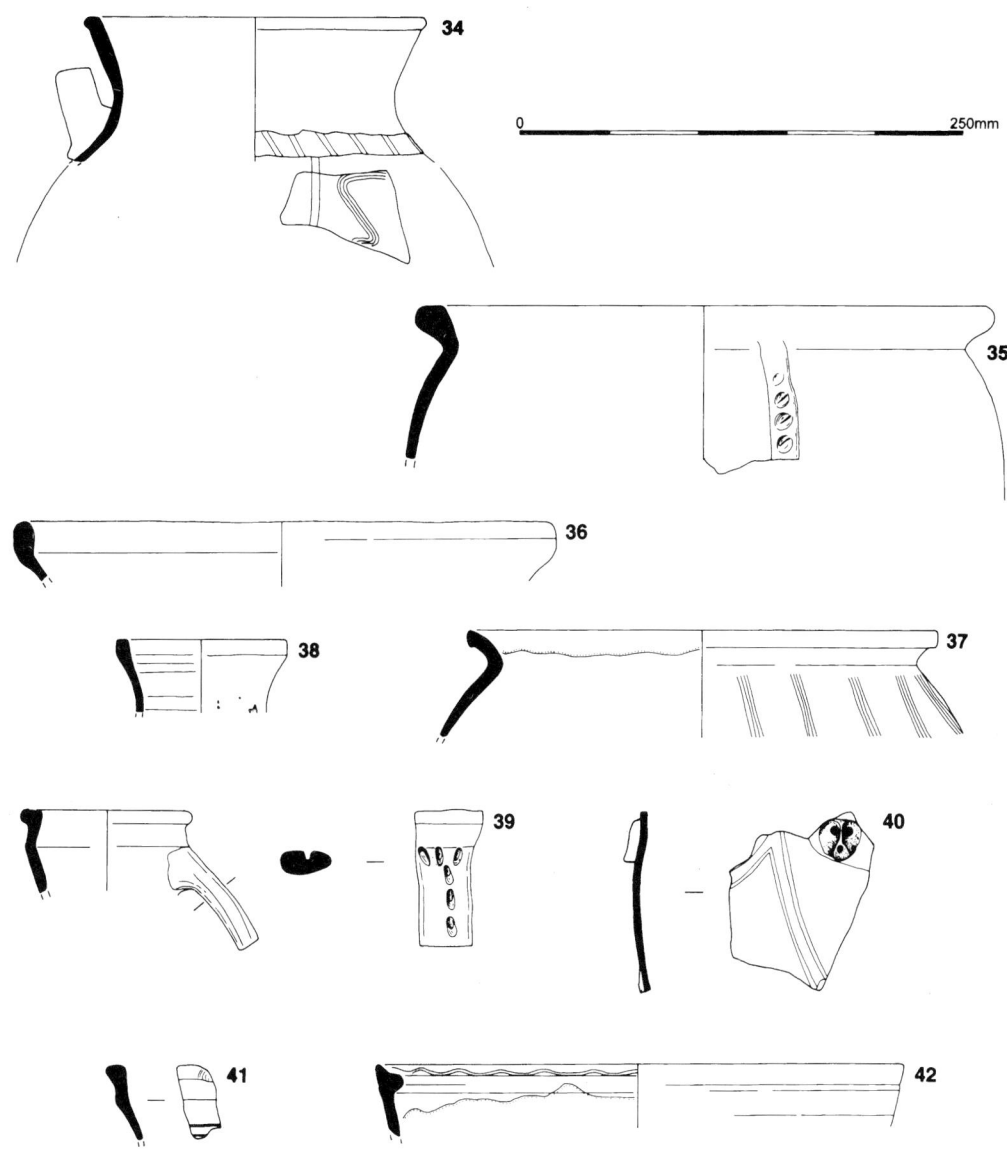

Fig. 15: Medieval pottery (scale 1:4)

Catalogue of illustrated wares (Figs 12–15)

8. St Neots-type ware dish. Layer 706.
9. Handmade jar with a wheel-turned rim. Mid brown with a lighter interior. Decorated with vertical applied thumb strips, an unusual feature for these wares, TF40. Late 12th to early 13th century. Layer 1185.
10. Five bodysherds from a Minety ware pitcher with an unusual decorative scheme of applied notched vertical strips, applied clay pellets and short combed lines, TF 44. Late 12th to 13th century. Layer 1194.
11. Handmade 'West Country dish', brown in colour with a wheel-finished rim, TF40. Fill 638 of pit 637.
12. Early Malvernian-type handmade jug (Hereford fabric B3) with a pulled spout and wheel-finished rim. Decorated with an applied frill around the neck and alternating bands of horizontal combing and wavy combed lines on the body. Reddish-fawn surfaces covered with a thin patchy light green glaze. Early–mid 13th-century type. Fill 761 of pit 760.
13. Handmade jar with wheel-finished rim. Light grey in colour, TF40. Fill 761 of pit 760.
14. Minety jug with a pulled spout and a small hole drilled through the upper body after firing. The exterior is decorated with combed lines and a partial light green glaze. The interior surface is leached. First half 13th century. Layer 404.
15. Handmade dark grey cooking pot with a sooted exterior, TF40. Layer 404.
16. Handmade jar with a wheel-finished rim. Dark grey sandy ware, TF42. Fill 615 of pit 611.
17. Jug with a strap handle, comb decorated. Possibly also with applied vertical ribs. Originally glazed but little evidence left, TF90. 13th century. Fill 1014 of pit 1013.
18. Handmade jar with a wheel-finished rim, TF42. Fill 732 of pit 731.
19. Handmade cooking pot, TF40 with a heavily sooted exterior. Fill 1072 of pit 1068.
20. Handmade jar, TF43. Later 12th to 13th century. Fill 1070 of pit 1068.
21. Handmade jar in black ware with dense oolitic limestone tempering, TF41B. Later 12th to 13th century. Fill 1070 of pit 1068.
22. Handmade/?wheel-turned jar with a club rim, TF40. Fill 1092 of pit 1091.
23. Handmade cooking pot, TF40 with a sooted exterior. Fill 1092 of pit 1091.
24. Wheelmade jar with an oxidised exterior, TF40. Fill 873 of ditch 858.
25. Wheelmade jar with a brownish-orange exterior, TF40. Late 13th to 14th century. Fill 1069 of pit 1068.
26. Handmade jar, TF40. Fill 1069 of pit 1068.
27. Handmade cooking pot with a sooted exterior, TF40. Late 13th to 14th century. Fill 1069 of pit 1068.
28. Bodysherd from a glazed decorated jug with a strap handle. The body has rouletted decoration and is covered with a mottled dark green glaze, TF90. Fill 1069 of pit 1068.
29. Wheelmade bowl with a vertical 'basket' handle. Brownish-green glazed on the lower interior surface. Sooting on exterior surface, TF52. Late 13th to 14th century. Fill 1069 of pit 1068.
30. Jug with a streaky olive green and brown exterior glaze. TF52. Fill 851 of feature 805.
31. Light grey handmade jar, TF40. Fill 851 of feature 805.
32. Handmade jar with a hole drilled through the neck after firing, TF40. Fill 835 of feature 805.
33. Jar with a handmade body and wheel-turned rim. Oxidised TF40. Mid–late 13th century. Layer 684.
34. Rim, broken spout and bodysherds from a Minety ware spouted pitcher. The vessel is decorated with horizontal thumbed strips, vertical raised ribs and combed wavy lines. The exterior is covered with a thin pale green glaze. Late 12th century type. Layer 1113.
35. Jar, dark orange in colour with a grey core and grey-brown interior. Handmade with a wheel-finished rim. Decorated with a vertical thumbed strip, TF43. Late 12th to 13th century. Layer 1113.
36. Handmade jar with a folded-over rim. Oxidised exterior, TF40. Late 13th to 14th century type. Layer 1113.
37. Handmade, Minety ware jar with a wheel-turned rim. Combed decoration. The inner rim surface is covered with a green glaze which is not apparent on the body, possibly due to leaching, TF44. Layer 303.
38. Malvernian jug with splatters of green glaze, TF52. Layer 303.
39. Worcestershire jug with a stabbed strap handle. Originally glazed but surface damaged through burning, TF90. Layer 303.
40. Four sherds from a dark green-glazed jug decorated with curvilinear raised ribs and an applied face, TF90. Layer 756.
41. Jug with a pulled spout. Light grey fabric with whitish surfaces and traces of a light green external glaze. Ham Green ware, TF53. Layer 756.
42. Rim from an OXY type dish decorated with a wavy line on the upper rim surface. Internal brownish green glaze. Layer 701/623.

Table 2: Total quantities of medieval fabrics
*: less than 1%; EVE: Estimated Vessel Equivalent

Source	Fabric	Name	No.	%	Wt (g)	%	EVE	%
Local	40	Malvern Chase cooking pot	1699	71	15,299	60	1164	66
	52	Malvern Chase glazed ware	257	11	4124	16	212	12
	MAL	Malvernian type (Hereford B3)	16	*	317	1	45	2.5
	42	Herefordshire sandy ware	154	6.5	1484	6	103	6
	90	Worcester-type jugs	81	3	1040	4	42	2
	WI	Winchcombe limestone-temper	3	*	31	*	0	0
Gloucester area	41	Gloucester early medieval ware	22	1	207	1	13	*
	43	Quartz and limestone	42	2	600	2	52	3
Wiltshire	44	Minety ware	99	4	2070	8	118	7
Oxon/Bucks	OXAM	Brill-Boarstall type	8	*	40	*	0	0
	OXY	Sandy Oxford ware	2	*	37	*	0	0
	BB	Brill-Boarstall	1	*	9	*	0	0
	OXR	St. Neots type	1	*	7	*	4	*
Avon	53	Ham Green jugs	8	*	49	*	2	*
Unknown	SX	Saxon	3	*	26	*	0	0
	MFE	Iron-tempered cooking pot	3	*	36	*	0	0
	M00	Miscellaneous	1	*	43	*	0	0
Total			2400	100	25,419	100	1755	100

Brick and Tile, by Emma Harrison

Period 2: Roman
A small abraded group of 91 fragments of brick and tile (17,648g) was recovered. The majority is Roman in date (78 fragments), although much of this was redeposited in medieval contexts. Fifty-one fragments (10,445g), including tegula, imbrex, flat and box tile, were reused in medieval cobbled surface 1111. The latter is indicative of a former hypocausted building in the vicinity.

Periods 4 to 5: Medieval and post-medieval
A small quantity of medieval roof tile was recovered, comprising one unglazed and four green-glazed fragments. Eight brick fragments were recovered from the primary fill of pit 1019, one of which had a 'B' stamped on the surface.

The Coins, by Peter Guest

Period 2: Roman
Five coins were recovered from the excavations. Four originated from ditch fill 847 and, of these, three could be dated to the fourth decade of the 4th century. These late Roman bronze coins found together probably formed part of a small hoard. The three identifiable coins are all of the common GLORIA EXERCITVS (1 and 2 standards) issues struck during the AD 300s. Their restricted date-range suggests these coins were buried together not long after the date of the most recent coin, which would have been some time between AD 340 and 350. One example from the hoard is possibly a contemporary forgery, suggesting a date of burial towards the later end of this decade.

Britain produces a significant peak of hoards containing coins from the AD 330s, all of which are composed of the bronze denominations such as the Stoke Road examples. An explanation of the widespread burial and loss of hoards at this date has yet to be put forward.

The small and very worn copper alloy coin from fill 857 of medieval pit 856 is residual, probably a barbarous radiate dating to the years AD 260–90.

Table 3: Catalogue of coins
    Denom: Denomination

Context	Obverse	Reverse	Denom.	Mint mark	Mint	Date (AD)
847	copper alloy coin	-	AE3	// [.....]	-	late 3rd to 4th C.
847	House of Constantine	GLORIA EXERCITVS 2 stds	AE3	// [.....]	-	330–37
847	House of Constantine	GLORIA EXERCITVS 1 std	AE3	o //[PCONST]	Arles	337–40
847	House of Constantine	GLORIA EXERCITVS 1 std	AE3	// [.....]	-	335–40
857	Barbarous radiate	No legend or figure visible	barb. rad.	-	-	260–90

The Waterlogged Wood, by Rowena Gale

Period 4: Medieval

A single piece of waterlogged wood from wattle-lined pit 1068 was identified to genus level. The sample consisted of roundwood, which appeared to taper at one end suggesting that it may have originated from the lower end of a stake. It was identified as *Prunus* sp. (cherry, blackthorn or bird cherry), measured 20mm in diameter and had nine annual growth rings.

The Leather, by Quita Mould

Period 4: Medieval

Two fragments from the forepart of a shoe sole of turnshoe construction were found in fill 1072 of wattle-lined pit 1068. The shoe sole had been worn, repaired and subsequently cut up to salvage reusable leather before being finally discarded, indicating it to be cobbling waste.

The Worked Stone, by Fiona Roe

Period 2: Roman objects

A residual fragment of quern or millstone, made from burnt red sandstone from the Upper Old Red Sandstone of the Forest of Dean/Wye Valley area, was recovered from (medieval) layer 726. This variety of stone was widely used during the whole of the Roman period, and has been found, for instance, at West Hill, Uley (Roe 1993, 199), Kingscote (Gutierrez and Roe 1998, 176), Great Witcombe (Bevan 1998, 109) and previously at Bishop's Cleeve (Roe 1998, 128). The fragment has too great a thickness to have been part of the Roman disc type of quern. This, and the wide spacing of the grooves on the grinding surface, about 18mm apart, suggest that it may have been part of a millstone.

Stone mortars are not often identified during excavation, though they must have been in frequent use. The fragment of a small mortar (also from layer 726; Fig. 16.1) has one surviving lug, and is made from a shelly and oolitic Jurassic limestone, probably obtained locally on Cleeve

Hill. Surprisingly few mortars made from oolitic limestone have been recorded, even in areas where suitable limestone was available. Only one other example is known from the Cotswolds, from Cirencester (Viner 1982, 103), and there are others from as far afield as Lamyatt Beacon in Somerset (Leech 1986, 282) and Richborough in Kent (Dunning 1968, 111).

Period 2: Roman building stone

A circular block with a rectangular hole cut into it, from ditch fill 648, has been interpreted as a post support. It is made from the local Inferior Oolite, most probably from nearby Cleeve Hill. Three large postpads with square socket holes, similarly made from Jurassic limestone, were found at Birdlip Quarry, Cowley (Roe 1999, 420). A similarly worked block of Ham stone was found at Ilchester in Somerset (Leach 1982, Fig. 106).

An ashlar block of the local Inferior Oolite from layer 806 may be either Roman or medieval in date, and could conceivably have been utilised in both periods. It has a groove of unknown purpose on one flat face. A similar building block from Birdlip Quarry, Cowley was grooved on three sides (Roe 1999, 420).

Period 4: Medieval objects

Two rotary quern fragments were recovered from cobbled surface 1111. One is made from Upper Old Red Sandstone quartz conglomerate. Another recent find made from quartz conglomerate is a millstone fragment from a medieval or post-medieval deposit at Street Farm, Latton, Wiltshire (Roe 1999, 417). The second quern, a smaller rotary, is made from May Hill Sandstone, obtained either from May Hill itself or the Malverns. This hard Silurian grit was used little during the Roman period, although it had been popular for Iron Age saddle querns. May Hill sandstone seems to have staged something of a comeback in post-Roman and medieval times, however, and other known medieval finds include a rotary quern from Moreton-in-Marsh (Langton *et al.* 2000, 21).

A complete spindlewhorl from layer 686 was made from a fine-grained clay limestone, in the form of Lias, which was available locally at Bishop's Cleeve. Spindlewhorls are a somewhat universal object as far as typology is concerned, and the one from layer 686 is not unlike another from the Anglo-Saxon cemetery at Bishop's Cleeve (Holbrook 2000, Fig. 10).

Period 4: Medieval building stone

The stone roof slates recovered from the site are all rectangular in shape, and are thus medieval rather than Roman. They are made from a fissile, sandy, Jurassic limestone, which consists mainly of small shell fragments. There are old slate quarries on Sevenhampton Common (Richardson 1929, 106), some 9km from Bishop's Cleeve, which may have been the source for the roofing slates.

The Metalwork, by Jane Bircher

Only identifiable objects relating to a period are detailed here. All unstratified and unidentifiable objects are detailed in the archive, including an unstratified heraldic horse-harness pendant dating to the late 13th or early 14th century. A catalogue and description of all nails recovered is also lodged in the archive. No significant conclusions could be drawn from the types of nails represented or from their distribution across the site, and those nails which are from contexts which contain Roman pottery are not of Roman type (cf. Manning 1985, 134–7).

With the exception of the residual Anglo-Saxon strap-end (no. 1), a number of iron objects of unclear function and/or date (listed in the archive) and the cruciform fitting (no. 12) which is likely to be of later date, all the metal finds from this site are consistent with a 12th to 14th-century date. There are no identifiably Roman objects.

Period 4: Medieval copper-alloy objects

1. Zoomorphic strap-end (Fig. 16.2) of well-known Anglo-Saxon type, flat with bowed out sides and tapering to a point. Two rivets survive in the bi-lobed split terminal, which was originally attached to a leather belt or strap. The front is decorated with two stylised eyes. The pointed terminal is slightly damaged and appears undecorated. The back is plain. Zoomorphic strap-ends can be dated to the 9th or 10th centuries AD, but by comparison with other examples this one probably belongs to the earlier part of this period. Similar strap-ends are published in Biddle 1990, 500–2, nos 1062–71, Fig. 126; Keen 1986 and Webster and Backhouse 1991, 233–5, nos 191–5. Length 31mm, maximum width 9.5mm, maximum thickness 3mm. Residual find from fill 761 of pit 760.
2. Bar-mount with pendent loop (Fig. 16.3, 4). The two detached elements almost certainly formed a single unit although they are made from visibly different alloys and the mount displays a higher standard of workmanship. The finely made bar with suspension loop (Fig. 16.3) is rectangular with a raised plain central panel and grooves with transverse hatching along each edge. There are two tiny rivets *in situ* in the central panel. At the bottom a narrow extension with an expanded and pierced terminal was bent back and attached to the lower rivet to form the suspension loop. This is now damaged. A very similar example from a 14th-century deposit at Billingsgate is published in Egan and Pritchard 1991 (215, no. 1164, Fig. 134). Length 22mm, width 5mm. The open trefoil was roughly stamped from sheet metal (Fig. 16.4). One lobe of the trefoil is flat on the outer edge, which may indicate where it was suspended although no wear is visible. Overall dimensions 16mm by 14mm, thickness 1mm. The mount and pendant formed one of a pair of attachments to a belt for the suspension of a purse (or possibly a knife scabbard). Similar mounts and pendants are published in Egan and Pritchard 1991 (215, nos 1164–7, Fig. 134 and 219, nos 1189–93, Fig. 138). An interesting discussion of the types and uses of purses appears in the same publication (342–57). Radiograph no. 725. Layer 711.
3. Lace-tag made of a rolled sheet of metal with a straight edge-to-edge seam, now open. Likely to be 14th to 15th century but possibly 13th century (cf. London, in Egan and Pritchard 1991, 281–90) or 16th to 17th century (cf. Canterbury, Marlowe Car Park, Garrard 1995, 1061, no. 623, Fig. 455). Length 36mm. Radiograph no. 725. Fill 990 of ditch 810. Not illustrated.
4. Fragment of fine round-sectioned wire with a pointed hooked terminal and broken at the other end. It is too small for positive identification but could be part of a twisted wire dress or hair accessory of the type published in Egan and Pritchard 1991 (296, no. 1467, Fig. 197). ?Medieval. Length 13mm, maximum width 5mm, diameter <1mm. Radiograph no. 725. Intrusive find from fill 681 of Roman ditch 680. Not illustrated.
5. Cast hook of round section, tapering towards each end. A raised ring approximately one third of its length from one end probably functioned as a stop separating the protruding hook from the 'tang' driven into a wall or timber. No medieval parallels have been found for this object. Overall dimensions 48mm by 34mm, maximum diameter 6.5mm. Radiograph no. 724. Fill 835 of pit 805. Not illustrated.

Period 4: Medieval iron objects

6. Part of the socket and blade of a barbed and socketed arrowhead with a central rib. It belongs to the London Museum Medieval Catalogue type 15, used for hunting or warfare (Ward Perkins 1967, 65–73). Length 28mm. Radiograph nos 727, 729. Fill 1150 of ditch 1149. Not illustrated.

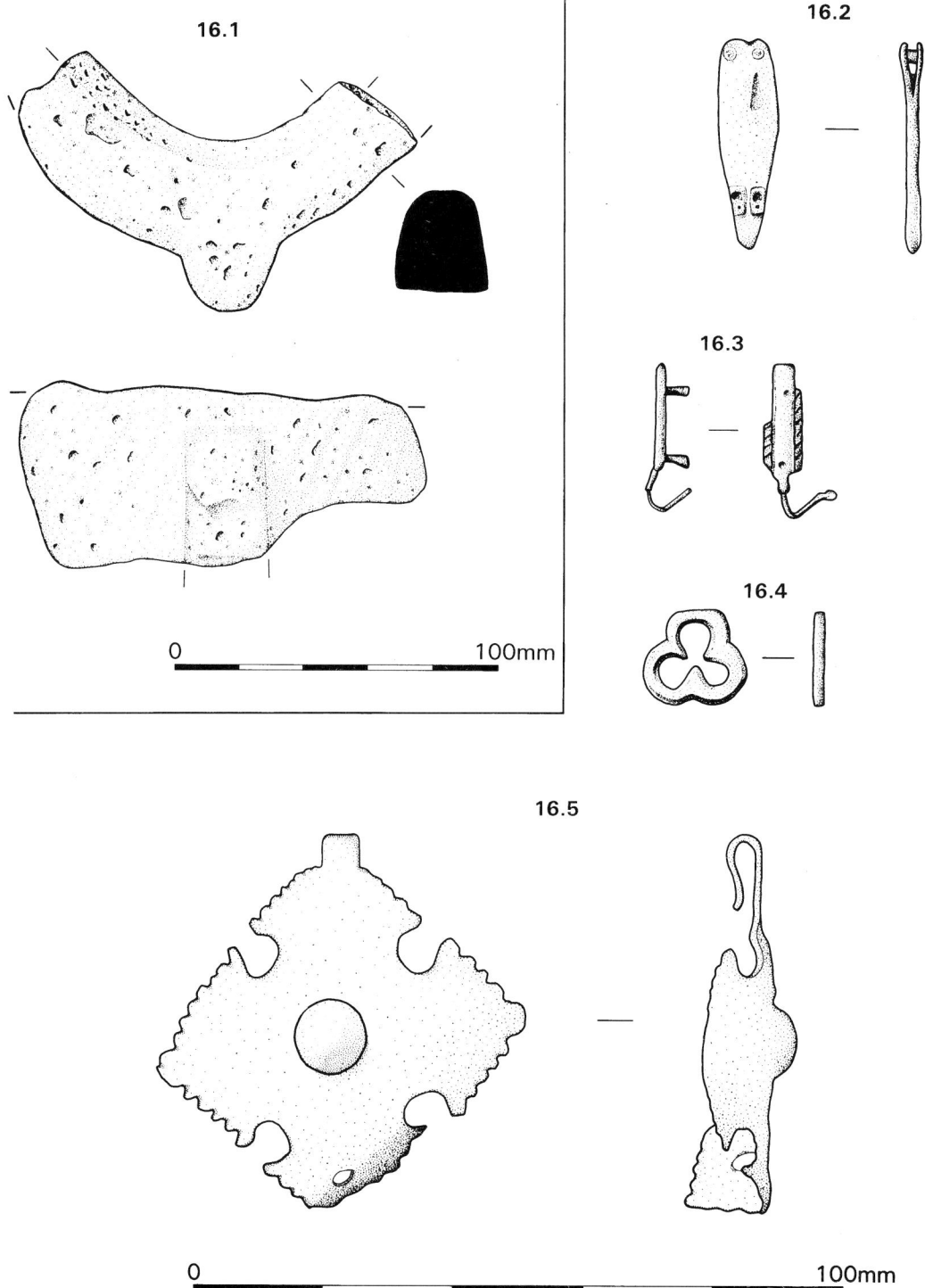

Fig. 16: Roman stone mortar fragment (inset: scale 1:2) and medieval and post-medieval copper alloy objects (scale 1:1)

7. Pin with ring head of rectangular section, widening above the point to a maximum thickness just below the looped head. The ring head is formed like a closed shepherd's crook. Pins with ring heads have been in use as simple locking devices from the Iron Age to the present. See Partridge 1981, 114–15, nos 77–9 for a discussion of their function. Length 79mm, width (ring) 16mm. Radiograph no. 727. Fill 1126 of ditch 1125. Not illustrated.
8. Fragment of the branch of a horseshoe with a folded calkin and three rectangular nail holes extant. It belongs to Museum of London type 3 (Clark 1995, 86–8 and 96, nos 144–89, Figs 83–5), dating to the 13th to 14th century. Length 91mm, maximum width 29mm. Radiograph no. 729. Layer 1112. Not illustrated.
9. Two horseshoe nails with expanded heads and ears for use with a type 3 horseshoe (see above). Both have their points missing. Extant lengths 34mm and 36mm. Radiograph no. 729. Layer 1112.
10. Large staple of square section with a flattened head. For structural use. Length 33mm, width 30mm. Radiograph no. 729. Layer 1112. Not illustrated.
11. Probable head of large staple of rectangular section. For structural use. Length 58mm, width 10mm, thickness 5mm. Radiograph no. 729. Layer 1112. Not illustrated.

Period 5: Post-medieval objects

12. Cruciform fitting cut from a square of sheet copper-alloy metal with an extension at one corner forming a bent back loop with an expanded terminal (Fig. 16.5). There is a round hole in the opposite corner. The decoration consists of a raised hollow boss in the centre and the edges are denticulated. A rounded notch in the middle of each side gives the cruciform shape. No medieval parallels have been found for this object which appears to be the fixed component of a hinged clasp for a book or casket. Probably post-medieval. Overall dimensions 44mm², thickness <1mm. Radiograph no. 725. Intrusive find from fill 761 of medieval pit 760.
13. Two iron horseshoes of similar type and size, possibly from the same animal. The oval shape of the shoes suggests that they came from the hind feet. Both have raised toes, no calkins and eight rectangular nail holes with some nails *in situ*. These nails are clenched which indicates that the shoes were thrown rather than removed by a farrier. They do not belong to a medieval type (cf. Clark 1995, 75–123). Post-medieval or modern. i) length 133mm, width 138mm; ii) length 133mm, width 133mm. Radiograph no. 728. Fill 921 of pit 920, which also contained horse remains. Not illustrated.

Discussion

The medieval copper-alloy objects are all indicative of individuals and activities of at least moderate status. The majority are small items of personal adornment or components of easily portable objects and except for the hook (no. 5) none are household fittings or objects used in domestic activity. All could therefore represent casual losses by people living in the area or passing through. The iron objects (if medieval) are all fairly insignificant and in keeping with the low status features on the site.

Metalworking Debris, by Chris Salter

Introduction

To obtain the distribution of slag types for the site, all the slag was classified by visual examination. Most of the metallic iron within the slag was identified by eye and then confirmed using a small hand-held metal detector, but some of the heavily slagged iron was only identified due to the use of the metal detector. A small number of pieces of slag and iron were selected for sectioning and polishing for further examination under the optical microscope. A full catalogue of the debris examined can be found in the archive.

The metalworking debris

A total of just over 22kg of material was examined, the majority of which came from contexts dating to the Roman period, with a minor amount of material coming from medieval contexts. Table 4 gives a breakdown of the weights of the various classes of material. All of the metallurgical material examined was likely to be the result of iron-smithing activity. There was no evidence of iron-smelting and although a few pieces of ironstone capable of being used as an iron ore were found, these were almost certainly natural occurrences.

In terms of weight the predominant material was smithing hearth bottoms and fragments from broken hearth bottoms, which made up 64% of the total weight. Thirty-five came from Roman contexts, eight from medieval contexts and eleven from unstratified or undated contexts. It is not clear whether this distribution represents two different periods of ironworking or the redeposition of Roman metalworking debris. However, only one smithing hearth bottom (slag no. 3863), a surface find, showed any extensive abrasion and it is very unlikely that the Roman slag could have been disturbed and redeposited after several hundred years without any obvious additional surface damage. The most likely interpretation is that there were two separate periods of ironworking.

The weight frequency histogram for the Roman and medieval complete or near complete smithing hearth bottoms is given in Table 5. It can be seen that although the number of hearth bottoms from the two periods were very different the weight frequency distributions fit the same pattern. The mean of the weights was 251g for Roman contexts and 223g for medieval contexts. The overall range of weights recorded was larger for those from Roman contexts. This is not considered significant as this distribution pattern seems normal for general smithing operations on charcoal-fuelled smithing sites. The majority of the welding activity results in the production of small hearth bottoms with weights under 500g, and the occasional larger hearth bottom is the result of the welding of a more substantial object, or the working up of a very slaggy piece of raw metal. The total debris recovered shows that a blacksmith's hearth had been used between twenty and thirty-four times in the Roman period, but only four to eight times during the medieval period. Considering the known loss of material due to disintegration of hearth bottoms through corrosion these figures are a poor indication of the minimum amount of ironworking activity.

No coal was found on this site, which contrasts with the evidence from the nearby Home Farm site, where there was definite evidence for a coal-fuelled forge during the 2nd century (Salter 1998). It would appear that the use of coal was abandoned here during the later part of the 2nd or early 3rd century and this could have been due either to the cost of transporting the coal from the Forest of Dean or to the artisan's preferences.

The metallic iron

Seven samples of metallic iron from Roman metalworking debris were sectioned, mounted in epoxy resin and prepared for metallographic examination. The results of these examinations are given in Table 6. Most of the metal was low carbon, and probably low phosphorus iron given the low hardness numbers recorded. Only one sample had an appreciable carbon content (s1008), and could have made an acceptable cutting edge. A number of pieces were overheated iron, or slagged iron which may have been generated by either the working of raw metal (slaggy bloom or billet), or by burning the metal by overheating during welding. None of the voids characteristic of bloom working were noted and there was clear evidence of welded stock. It is likely that these represent metal losses during welding and it would appear that there was higher than normal rate of metal lost at this site. This may have been due to the improved detection rate through the use of the metal detector, but as the debris of no smithing site has been quantitatively analysed for this sort of information there is a lack of comparative quantitative data.

All the metal was relatively soft and even that with an appreciable amount of carbon was in the lower part of the range that might be expected. This indicates that the metal was not cold

Table 4: Major classes of metallurgical debris by period
All weights in grammes

Debris type	2nd/4th C.	Medieval	Undated	Total weight
Fired clay	7.5	-	-	7.5
Hearth lining	211.1	76.3	138.4	-
Hearth lining/slag	1367.1	128.3	37.5	1532.9
Ironworking slag	4172.2	845.3	577.3	5594.8
Smithing hearth bottom complete	8769.8	1784.2	2625.6	13,179.6
Smithing hearth bottom fragment	861.7	117	188.8	1167.5
Metallic iron	168.2	12.6	-	180.8
Ore	6.9	14.2	-	21.1
Natural rock etc.	36.9	-	-	36.9
Modern non metallurgical	-	7.4	-	7.4
Non metallurgical soil etc.	9.2	124.5	83	216.7
Total weight	15,610.6	3109.8	3650.6	22,371

worked and is not surprising considering that the majority of the pieces were offcuts and that the cutting process would have been carried out hot, as was illustrated by sample s1005. The low hardness of the samples and the lack of phosphorus 'ghosting' suggest that the metal was non-phosphoritic, and thus likely to have come from the Forest of Dean (although compositional analysis would be required to confirm this suggestion).

The use of welded stock suggests the smith doubled up bar thicknesses by welding rather than forging out thicker stock. This implies that the smith was reusing scrap metal rather than new metal.

Table 5: Relative weight frequencies of Roman and medieval smithing hearth bottoms

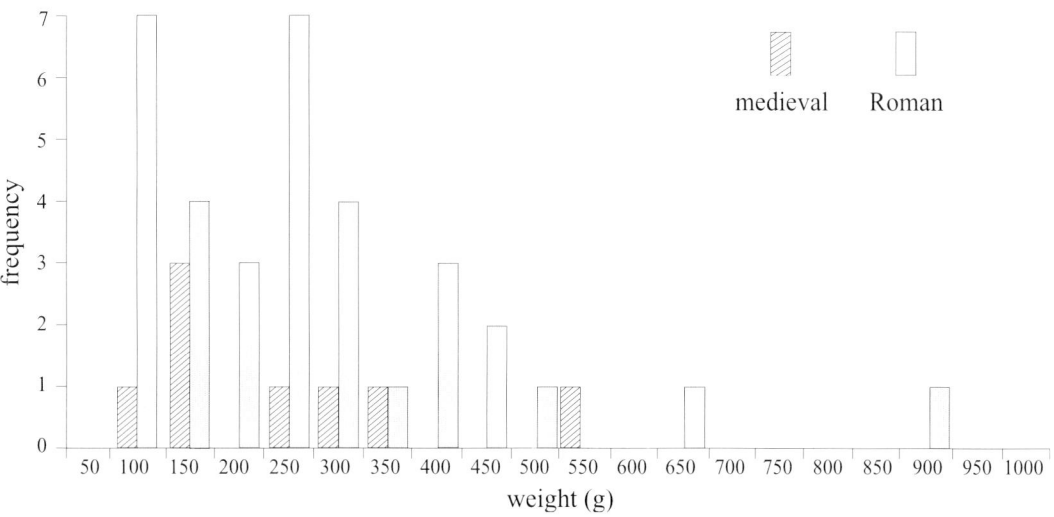

Table 6: *Metallographic examination of some of the fragments from the ironworking debris*

Context	Sample/slag no.	Description	Object type	Metallurgy
fill 648 (slot 647)	1009/s3863	Short section of bar with clear set cut marks at ends. On sectioning only a small strip remained.	Offcut	Remaining strip was a low carbon metal with a small amount of grain-boundary carbides. The hardnesses were between 123 and 153 VPN 2.5kg. May be phosphoritic.
layer 745	1008/s3998	Appeared to be an irregular length of bar. On sectioning it would seem that there was a central weld (as with sample 1006) but in this case one half has been completely corroded.	Strip	Variable carbon content ranging from less than 0.15% wt to 0.75% wt carbon. Hardness values from 89 to 180 VPN 5kg. In the high carbon regions the structure was of fine to moderate pearlite with widmanstätten ferrite. Air-cooled.
fill 784 (ditch 635)	1005/s3924	Irregular fragment of slagged iron.	Slagged metal	Ferritic iron with many oxide slag inclusions. Hardness between 99 and 107 VPN 5kg.
fill 815 (pit 814)	1006/s3852	Cut-off from welded bar with cut marks at both ends. At one end two blows were required to cut through the bar.	Offcut	In the main the metal was ferritic, but below the weld there was a region of 0.2 to 0.1 % wt carbon iron. Grain boundary cracking was present near the cuts, and stress corrosion cracking at the root of the partial cut. Hardness 89-117 VPN 5kg.
fill 834 (gully 833)	1010/s4032	Small fragment.	Offcut Slagged metal	Very slaggy soft metal with no carbon. Hardness 87-91 VPN 2.5kg.
fill 847 (ditch 632)	1007/s3924	Irregular fragment.	Fragment	Very slaggy ferrite. Hardness 93-109 VPN 5kg.
fill 847 (ditch 632)	1011/s3924	Irregular fragment: burnt metal.	Fragment	Very slaggy ferrite, with one region of iron oxide-metallic iron dendritic eutectic structure. Single hardness of 110 VPN 2.5kg.

Summary

The metalworking debris indicates that there were probably two periods of general small-scale ironworking, the first during the later Roman period in the 3rd to 4th century, and the second at some time during the 12th to 14th century. The activity was likely to have been simple artefact fabrication and repair for domestic and agricultural purposes. Although more slag was recovered than from many rural Romano-British sites, where the recovery of 1–5kg is quite normal, the amount is still relatively low and only represents 20–30 forge-days operation. The pieces of iron examined metallographically show that there was a substantial metal loss during welding, which may indicate that the smith was not used to welding. The slags and the fragmentary iron from a number of sites need to be analysed in detail however, before we can determine what was the normal rate of loss during welding. At the moment, this has not been done for any site of any period in Britain.

THE BIOLOGICAL EVIDENCE

The Human Remains, by Jacqueline McKinley

Introduction

Human bone was analysed from five contexts. Two contexts, 642 (Burial A) and 645 (Burial B), represented the *in situ* remains of Romano-British inhumation burials and a probable third grave contained disarticulated human bone (within fill 786: henceforth referred to as Burial C). Other bone was recovered from a ditch fill and from a gully fill. All of the contexts containing human bone were within a 10 x 6m area in the south-east quarter of the site.

Methods

Age was assessed from the stage of tooth development (Van Beek 1983) and ossification/epiphyseal bone fusion (Gray 1977; McMinn and Hutchings 1985; Webb and Suchey 1985), assessment of the sternal-end ossification in the ribs (Iscan *et al.* 1984), tooth wear patterns (Brothwell 1972) and the general degree of other age-related changes to the bone (e.g. Bass 1987). Sex was ascertained from the sexually dimorphic traits of the skeleton (Bass 1987). Platymeric and platycnemic indices were calculated according to Bass (1987). Stature was estimated using Trotter and Gleser's regression equations (1952, 1957). Pathological lesions and morphological variations were recorded and diagnoses suggested where appropriate. Anatomical terminology accords with Gray (1977) and McMinn and Hutchings (1985). Full details of all identified bone are presented in the archive report.

Results

A summary of the results is presented in Table 7.

Disturbance and condition

The two graves from which *in situ* remains were recovered were both very shallow, with a maximum depth of 0.1m. There had been extensive post-depositional disturbance both in antiquity and more recently, probably as a result of ploughing. Two later Romano-British linear features, each passing through different graves, had removed most of the skull from Burial B and were probably responsible for the redeposition of bone from Burial C some 2m to the west in gully fill 784 (though much of the bone from this burial was not recovered at all). In Burial A, the loss of much of the lower leg and feet bones (fragments of fibula and metatarsal were recovered) was probably due to removal by ploughing. The short grave length suggests the legs may have been bent back under the body or, possibly, flexed to one side.

The bone was generally in good condition, though there was some exfoliation of cortical bone in the long bone shafts from Burial A. The bone from both *in situ* burials was badly shattered, presumably in consequence of the shallow depth of the graves and associated plough damage. All of the disarticulated bone was slightly battered in appearance, with some old, post-depositional cut marks in bone from fill 650 and Burial C.

Several fragments of bone from Burial C (parietal vault, left pelvis and femur shaft) have black staining over one or both surfaces (external/internal) and over the broken surfaces. This may represent sooting, and clearly occurred post-depositionally and once the bone was already broken. A small area of iron-staining on the left radius shaft from Burial B indicates the former presence of an iron object in the grave.

Skeletal indices and morphology
No intact crania were recovered. Stature was estimated for the two adult males using the ulna (the only intact long bone); Burial B was estimated at 1.86m and Burial C at 1.76m. Both measurements are within the upper range of estimated heights recorded for males from Cirencester (Wells 1982) and Poundbury (Molleson 1993). Platymeric (degree of anterior-posterior flattening of the proximal femur) and platycnemic indices (meso-lateral flattening of the tibia) could be calculated only for Burial B, giving eurymeric and eurycnemic readings.

Both adult males were of robust build with strong muscle attachments. This was particularly noticeable in Burial B, where attachments in the femora, humeri and ulnae were particularly pronounced, with a bias towards the right in the forearm (*pronator quadratus* and *flexor digitorim profundus*).

Demographic data
The remains of four individuals were identified: a young subadult (*c.* 13–15 years), two mature adults (*c.* 25–45 years) and one older mature/older adult (>30 years). Two of the adults were male, the other adult probably female and the subadult possibly female. The presence of human bone in ditch fill 650, redeposited from an unlocated grave, is indicative of the probable existence of more graves in the vicinity, possibly completely ploughed away. The presence of both sexes and both immature and adult individuals within the assemblage, small and possibly incomplete though it may be, suggests a 'normal' domestic-type cemetery attached to a small settlement/farmstead.

Pathological lesions and morphological variations
The limited size of the group and incomplete skeletal recovery as a result of disturbance precludes any general comment on health status. The extensive lesions noted in Burial B are most probably reflective of the age of the individual.

DENTAL DISEASE
Mild-medium dental calculus was observed in all dentitions (covering about one-quarter to one-third of the crown), as was a low degree of periodontal disease (gum infection). Only one tooth was lost *ante mortem* (2%), from one of the adult male dentitions. Carious lesions were noted in one female and one male dentition, with an overall rate of 5.4% (5.9% female, 5% male), and in both cases lesions were in the maxillary molars. In the adult male, the infection from the carious lesion had tracked into the tooth socket resulting in the development of the only dental abscess noted in the assemblage (1.9% overall, 2.8% male). There was a noticeably low level of tooth wear, particularly in the older adult male, where the pattern of attrition was commensurate with those of a young adult (Brothwell 1972, 69).

The rates of dental disease are comparatively low and are most closely comparable with those recorded by Wells from Cirencester (1982), 5.1% caries and 1.2% abscesses, though the rate of *ante mortem* tooth loss was higher at 8.5%. A general rate of 9.3% for carious lesions within Romano-British groups has been quoted by Molleson (1993). Such low rates may signify a high level of nutrition with a diet based predominantly on meat or fish, probably supported by a relatively good level of dental hygiene, though the small size of the assemblage means the results should be treated with caution.

In Burial C infection had spread from the maxillary dental abscess superiorly into the antrum and buccally to the external surface of the maxilla. This had resulted in secondary sinusitis (Wells

1977) and infection of the soft tissues of the cheek. Periosteal new bone was noted on the ventral surface of at least three bodies of the sacrum in the subadult Burial A. This is indicative of some form of infection within the adjacent soft tissues.

JOINT DISEASE

Osteophytes are irregular growths of new bone that may develop along joint margins, the prevalence increasing with age, or in association with other lesions where they may be indicative of disease such as osteoarthritis (Rogers and Waldron 1995). A limited number of lesions were noted in Burial C, while lesions were noted at about 38 sites in Burial B.

Table 7: *Summary of results from human bone analysis*
   % rec.: percentage skeleton recovered in inhumation burial

```
KEY TO PATHOLOGY
pd:    periodontal disease       mv:   morphological variation      C:     cervical
c-v:   costo-vertebral           ddd:  degenerative disc disease    amtl:  ante mortem tooth loss
T:     thoracic                  oa:   osteoarthritis               pnb:   periosteal new bone
Sch:   Schmorl's nodes           L:    lumbar                       ap:    articular process
dl:    destructive lesions       op:   osteophytes                  S:     sacral
bsm:   body surface margins      exo:  exostoses                    p:     proximal
IP:    inter-phalangeal          d:    distal                       r/l:   right/left
```

Context	Type	% rec.	Age	Sex	Pathology	Comment
Burial A (642)	*in situ* burial	*c.* 50%	subadult (*c.* 13-14yr)	?female	calculus; pnb - ventral sacrum; mv - 3rd distal centres ossification 1st metacarpals	
Burial B (645)	*in situ* burial	*c.* 70%	adult (30yr +)	male	pd; calculus; amtl; oa - l.pisiform-triquetral, l.shoulder, r.1st metacarpal-phalangeal, C4, 1L, S1, min. 1/9-12 c-v; ddd - C3-7, T6-7, T12, 4L, S1; Sch. - T7-12 op - r. scapula, d.humeri, p.radii and ulnae, r.d.ulna l.lunate and trapezium, all proximal and distal IP (finger), femoral heads, l.d.tibia, auricular surfaces, acetabulae, T ap, T5-12 bsm, 4 L bsm, 3L ap, S1 bsm and ap, 3 l. and 6 r.rib facets, l.navicular; new bone - proximal phalanx (contours lost); pitting - l.d.tibia, acetabulae; exo. - proximal finger phalanx, r.acromion, p.femurs, iliac crest, ischial tuberosities, l.4th metatarsal shaft, r.1st proximal foot phalanx	Fe stain left radius shaft
650	redep. ditch	*c.* 1%	adult (*c.* 25-45yr)	female	caries; pd; calculus; op - L	pig bone
784	redep. gully	*c.* 12%	adult (*c.* 25-45yr)	male	calculus; pd; mv - congenital absence mandibular M3	=786
Burial C (786)	dist. burial	*c.* 25%	adult (*c.* 25-45yr)	male	calculus; pd; caries; abscess; pnb - maxilla; ?sinusitis; op - auricular surface, T/L bsm; pitting - l.m.clavicle, S1 ap; exo. - r.olecranon; d.l. - S1	=784

Degenerative disc disease is represented by pitting in the vertebral body surfaces following the breakdown of the intervertebral disc. The condition is largely related to age and reflects 'wear-and-tear'. Lesions were noted in ten vertebrae from Burial B (rate 42%). The same individual had Schmorl's nodes in six vertebrae (rate 25%); these destructive lesions result from a rupture in the intervertebral disc allowing the nucleus pulposus to protrude into the vertebral body.

Osteoarthritis, a disease of the synovial joints, is manifest by eburnation of the joint surface and/or pitting in association with osteophytes on the surface margins. The aetiology is complicated, including the effects of age, mechanical alteration through activity or injury and genetic predisposition (Rogers and Waldron 1995). Of the lesions noted at 11 sites in Burial B, none was severe.

Pitting and other destructive lesions may develop in response to a number of conditions and it is not always possible to ascertain specific cause (Rogers and Waldron 1995). The vast majority were seen in joint surfaces, with others peri- or juxta-articular, and are most likely to represent the early stages of some form of joint disease. Similarly it is not always possible to be conclusive with respect to the aetiology of exostoses (bony growths which may develop at tendon and ligament insertions on the bone). Causative factors include advancing age, traumatic stress, or various diseases.

One unsided proximal (?foot) phalanx from Burial B has lesions in the head suggestive of infection within the joint; the contours of the head had been totally remodelled, being covered by uneven new bone extending out from the surface, especially on the planter and posterior sides and slightly down the posterior surface of shaft (15.5mm planter-posterior, 13.9mm medial-lateral). No lesions were noted in other adjacent bones to aid diagnosis.

The Animal Bone, by Mark Maltby

Method

All animal bones were recorded individually onto a database, which forms part of the site archive. Where appropriate, the following information was recorded on each fragment: context; feature; period; species; anatomy; part of bone present; proportion of bone present; gnawing damage; surface condition; fusion data; tooth ageing data; butchery marks; metrical data; other comments. Where necessary, identifications were confirmed by reference to the comparative skeleton collection housed in the School of Conservation Sciences, Bournemouth University. Toothwear descriptions followed the method of Grant (1982). Measurements are those recommended by von den Driesch (1976) with a few additions.

Bones from sieved samples were counted separately from those recovered by normal excavation. In both cases only specimens identified to species were recorded in detail. Approximate counts for rib shafts, peripheral parts of vertebrae and other fragments not identified to species in each context can be found in the archive.

Period 2: Roman (Table 8)

Normal excavation produced a sample of 139 identified fragments from deposits dating to the Roman period. Most were derived from ditches but 77 bones belonging to partial sheep skeletons came from pit 621. Most of the bones from pit 621 belonged to two sheep: a fully grown adult animal was represented by most of the major bones of the forelimb, the left femur and the proximal halves of both tibiae, and a younger sheep was represented by (at least) both humeri and radii, the left ulna, the right metacarpal, both femora, patellae and tibiae and the right metatarsal. The early fusing limb bone epiphyses had fused but the distal ends of the metapodials were unfused and the distal tibia was just fusing, suggesting this sheep died probably in its second year. In addition, a third sheep was represented by most of another right tibia with a fused distal epiphysis. This belonged to a sheep older than the second skeleton.

No evidence of butchery marks was found on any of the bones and their fragmentary condition is most likely to have been the result of post-depositional factors. However, there is no evidence that any of the bones had been gnawed, which suggests immediate burial. The significance of this group is enigmatic. They could have been ritual depositions but it is also possible that they were sheep that died of disease and whose meat was considered unsuitable for consumption.

Cattle were represented by 66 fragments, ten of which were from ditch 628 and belonged to the left forefoot of an adult animal. The greatest length of the metacarpal provided an estimated withers height of 1.21m and breadth measurements suggest it was from a male. Several of the bones in this group had abnormal extra growth of bone on the edge of the articular surfaces (lipping), perhaps indicative of an arthritic condition. Similar pathology was observed on six other cattle metapodials and phalanges, a relatively large incidence given the small sample size. A second complete metacarpal and a metatarsal provided estimated withers heights of 1.24m and 1.22m respectively and the large breadth measurements of these specimens again indicated that they probably belonged to steers or bulls. Several incomplete limb bones also produced relatively broad measurements, again perhaps indicating that they were from males (Grigson 1982).

Cattle ageing data were limited, but the assemblage contained bones mainly from adult cattle, in some cases quite elderly animals. For example, a mandible from pit 797 had heavy wear on its second and third molars and had suffered the ante-mortem loss of its first molar and fourth premolar, so was from a relatively old animal, as was an upper third molar from the same feature, which may have belonged to the same animal. A maxilla from ditch 616 also possessed a fully erupted tooth row. The high incidence of pathological bones also suggests the presence of a number of mature cattle.

The bias towards older, quite large and probably male cattle suggests that working animals, perhaps plough cattle, were well represented in these deposits. The pathological conditions may also have been at least partially caused by this activity in some cases.

Butchery marks were observed on four cattle bones. The mandible from pit 797 described above bore knife cuts on the buccal and lingual aspects below the cheek teeth (possibly made during the removal of the tongue); a humerus from ditch 707 bore superficial chop marks running across its shaft; a calcaneus from gully 787 bore similar marks on its lateral surface (probably made during segmentation of the carcass) and a metatarsal from ditch 603 bore knife cuts on its lateral aspect near the distal end, possibly made during the initial stages of skinning. None of these marks indicate the presence of specialist butchers, like those who left distinctive patterns of butchery marks on cattle bones in Cirencester (Maltby 1998).

Pig bones were very rare but two mandibles with early wear on their second molars indicate the presence of pigs slaughtered in their second year for meat. A much younger piglet was represented by a porous femur.

Horse bones were relatively well represented by 18 bones and teeth, in contrast to excavations in Cirencester, which have produced the low numbers of horse remains characteristic of urban assemblages (Maltby 1994; 1998). Horses represented on Romano-British sites are usually adult animals, indicating they were kept primarily for uses other than meat, but in this sample there were also two bones from immature horses: an unfused proximal epiphysis of a femur and an unfused proximal tibia, both from ditch 616. The tibia had a fused distal end, indicating death

Table 8: *Species and anatomies represented in Roman deposits*
S/G: sheep/goat; assoc. : associated cattle bones in ditch 628; Burials: sheep burials in pit 621; sieved: bones from sieved sample from pit 621

	Cattle assoc.	Cattle other	S/G burials	S/G sieved	S/G other	Pig	Horse	Dog	Red Deer
Maxilla	-	1	-	-	-	-	-	-	-
Other skull	-	4	1	-	1	-	2	-	-
Mandible	-	3	1	-	2	3	-	-	-
Loose teeth	-	8	-	-	6	-	2	-	-
Humerus	-	3	3	1	-	1	1	-	-
Radius	-	4	3	-	1	-	4	-	-
Ulna	-	1	1	2	-	-	-	-	-
Scapula	-	2	2	1	-	-	-	-	-
Pelvis	-	-	1	-	1	-	3	-	-
Femur	-	2	3	-	-	1	1	-	1
Patella	-	-	1	1	-	-	-	-	-
Tibia	-	4	5	-	1	-	1	-	-
Carpals	3	1	1	4	-	-	-	-	-
Astragalus	-	-	1	-	-	-	1	-	-
Calcaneus	-	2	-	-	-	-	-	-	-
Centroquartal	-	-	1	-	-	-	-	-	-
Metacarpal	1	3	3	-	-	-	1	-	-
Metatarsal	-	5	1	-	1	-	1	-	-
Metapodial	-	-	-	-	-	-	1	-	-
1st Phalanx	2	3	1	3	-	-	-	-	-
2nd Phalanx	-	2	-	2	-	-	-	-	-
3rd Phalanx	2	2	-	-	-	-	-	-	-
Sesamoids	2	-	-	2	-	-	-	-	-
Ribs	-	1	-	11	-	-	-	-	-
Axis	-	1	-	-	-	-	-	-	-
Cervical verts	-	3	2	-	-	-	-	-	-
Thoracic verts	-	-	3	14	-	-	-	-	-
Sacrum	-	1	-	-	-	-	-	-	-
Caudal verts	-	-	-	1	-	-	-	1	-
Sternebrae	-	-	-	1	-	-	-	-	-
Total	**10**	**56**	**34**	**43**	**13**	**5**	**18**	**1**	**1**

between two and four years old. It also bore butchery marks in the form of knife cuts running horizontally on various parts of the shaft. Evidence for the exploitation of horsemeat is less common on Romano-British sites than on Iron Age settlements but it has been found occasionally. A complete radius from ditch 603 belonged to a horse with an estimated withers height of 1.37m (13.5 hands).

The only dog bone identified was a cervical vertebra from ditch 616, although the presence of dogs on the settlement is attested by the presence of gnawed bones. A femur of a red deer from ditch 603 provided the only evidence for the exploitation of wild species. The absence of domestic fowl bones is not surprising. Even in substantially larger samples they have been found only in small numbers, if any, on most Romano-British non-villa rural settlements, although they were found in later Romano-British deposits at Home Farm (Maltby 1997).

Period 4: Medieval (Table 9)

Normal excavation produced a total of 263 bones identified to species. Of these, 25 were found in ditch fills, 76 in pits, 144 in layers and 18 in other types of context, mainly postholes. A small number of bones were also identified from the sieved samples.

Eighty of the bones from normal excavation bore gnawing marks, indicating that much of the assemblage had been accessible to dogs prior to final deposition. Sheep/goat was the most commonly identified category in all types of context, providing over half (140) of the total of identified bones. Generally, there was a bias towards bones of higher density such as the tibia, mandible and radius, but the assemblage from layer 701 included 39 sheep/goat metapodials and phalanges, indicating the disposal of complete feet detached from dressed carcasses, perhaps initially attached to the skins.

The importance of sheep in the Cotswolds in the medieval period, particularly for wool production, is well known and their abundance in archaeological deposits here is unsurprising. Although preservation factors will have biased the sample against the recovery of bones of younger animals, it is nevertheless notable that the majority of the ageable bones and teeth were from adult animals. Out of eleven mandibles with surviving cheek teeth, six belonged to sheep of at least four years of age and a seventh was probably from an individual that died in its third or fourth year. Of the remainder, three mandibles belonged to sheep which were probably slaughtered for meat between eighteen and twenty-four months and the last jaw belonged to a lamb that died at about a year old. The less reliable epiphysial fusion evidence also indicated that both immature and adult sheep were represented. The older animals would have produced several fleeces of wool prior to slaughter for mutton, reflecting that wool was the major factor in sheep exploitation at that time.

Three complete metacarpals from layer 701 and a metatarsal from pit 1203 belonged to sheep with estimated withers heights of approximately 0.49m, 0.51m, 0.56m and 0.50m respectively. Several of the sheep represented were therefore very small stock and appear to have been generally smaller than the Romano-British sheep found on the site. Small types of sheep have been noted in a number of earlier medieval samples, for example in York (O'Connor 1991) and Exeter (Maltby 1979), but it is of interest that many slightly larger sheep were represented in deposits in Gloucester that were contemporary with those at Bishop's Cleeve (Maltby 1983).

Cattle bones were less well represented than in the Romano-British deposits but nevertheless accounted for 28% of the identified sample from normal excavation. Parts of the head, particularly mandibles and loose teeth, and feet, mainly metapodials, were the best represented elements.

Tooth wear analysis and limited epiphyseal fusion evidence revealed the presence of cattle of various ages ranging from new born calves to mature animals. No evidence of pathology was recorded on any of the bones, but butchery marks were observed on eight cattle bones and included a skull fragment from pit 654 that had been chopped through to remove the brain. Three mandibles bore chop marks on the ascending ramus made during separation from the skull and another mandible had a knife cut on the lingual aspect of the diastema, perhaps

Table 9: Species and anatomies represented in medieval deposits
Counts exclude bones in sieved samples. S/G: sheep/goat; Fowl: domestic fowl; Goose: domestic goose

	Cattle	S/G	Pig	Horse	Dog	Fallow Deer	Fowl	Goose
Maxilla	2	2	-	2	-	-	-	-
Other Skull	2	-	-	-	1	-	-	-
Mandible	14	15	2	4	-	-	-	-
Loose Teeth	11	12	4	3	-	-	-	-
Humerus	5	6	1	-	1	-	-	-
Radius	3	12	1	-	1	-	-	-
Ulna	1	1	2	-	1	-	-	-
Scapula	2	-	1	-	-	-	-	-
Coracoid	-	-	-	-	-	-	2	-
Pelvis	3	2	-	-	-	-	-	-
Femur	3	4	1	-	-	-	-	-
Tibia	4	23	3	1	-	-	-	-
Fibula	-	-	1	-	-	-	-	-
Carpals	1	-	-	-	-	-	-	-
Astragalus	-	2	1	-	-	-	-	-
Calcaneus	1	1	-	-	-	-	-	-
Centroquartal	1	-	-	-	-	1	-	-
Other tarsals	-	-	-	1	-	-	-	-
Metacarpal	6	15	1	1	-	1	-	-
Metatarsal	6	19	-	1	-	2	1	1
Metapodial	1	-	-	-	-	-	-	-
1st Phalanx	6	11	1	1	-	-	-	-
2nd Phalanx	1	9	-	2	-	-	-	-
3rd Phalanx	-	6	-	-	-	-	-	-
Atlas	-	-	1	-	-	-	-	-
Axis	-	-	-	-	1	-	-	-
Cervical verts	1	-	-	-	-	-	-	-
Thoracic verts	-	-	-	-	-	-	-	-
Total	74	140	20	16	5	4	3	1

associated with the removal of the tongue. A knife cut was observed also on the sacro-iliac joint of a pelvis. A scapula from pit 746 had been chopped through across the blade during segmentation of the carcass. Finally, a centroquartal bore a horizontal knife cut on its medial aspect made during the removal of the feet.

Only twenty pig bones were identified and included a radius, metacarpal and first phalanx from pit 611 which probably belonged to the same immature animal. All three bones had been burnt. A tibia had been chopped through its shaft near the proximal end when the carcass was segmented.

Horse was represented by at least 16 fragments, nearly all from the head and feet, and no bones or teeth of immature horses were recorded. No evidence of carcass processing was found.

A complete metacarpal from pit 780 provided an estimated withers height of approximately 1.38m. Five dog bones were identified including most of a skull from ditch 980.

The medieval assemblage included a slightly wider range of species than the Romano-British sample. Four fallow deer bones were identified including a centroquartal and metatarsal from the same animal in pit 1064. Their presence indicates the exploitation of game species but their contribution to the diet appears negligible compared with assemblages from some castle and manor sites, for example, Launceston Castle in Cornwall (Albarella and Davis 1996). Bird species were also limited to domestic varieties, three bones of domestic fowl (chicken) and one of goose being the only ones identified.

Period 5: Post-medieval
Animal bones recorded from pit fill 921 included thirty-four bones belonging to an adult horse skeleton. All bones of the shoulder and forelimbs were recovered apart from the left metacarpal and most of the carpals and sesamoids. Eight ribs, four cervical and five thoracic vertebrae of this skeleton were also recovered. All the bones were fused and belonged to an adult animal of between 1.46m and 1.53m according to estimates derived from length measurements. The horse was therefore significantly larger than the Romano-British and medieval specimens recovered. A humerus and the radius of a small dog (shoulder height estimated at *c.* 0.3m) were found in the same pit. The shaft of the radius was distorted and had extra growth of bone on its lateral aspect, perhaps resulting from a traumatic injury.

Conclusions
The faunal assemblage was very small and can provide only limited insights into animal exploitation on the site, but the Romano-British sample appears to be fairly typical of a non-villa rural assemblage, with a restricted range of species exploited and hints that plough cattle may have been kept. Sheep appear to have been the most commonly exploited species in the medieval period, with wool probably the most important commodity.

The Ecofactual Evidence, by Julie Jones and David Smith

Introduction
A total of 12 bulk samples (◇) was taken for palaeoenvironmental examination during the excavation. These were from a variety of features of both Roman and medieval date, however, following initial assessment no samples from features of Roman date were considered for detailed analysis. Of the medieval samples selected for detailed analysis, samples ◇6, ◇9 and ◇10 were from waterlogged features and the remainder from others that appeared rich in charred plant remains (Table 10).

It was hoped that palaeoenvironmental analysis could provide evidence for the function of the pits sampled, indicate something of the environment in which the medieval population lived, and provide evidence of economy and diet. As preservation of biological remains from medieval rural sites in Gloucestershire is extremely rare (there are at present no published examples where waterlogged remains have been found), the floral and faunal assemblages at Bishop's Cleeve are of considerable importance.

In addition, two monolith samples (◇11) were taken through deposits within a depression at the southern end of the site: these results are described separately below (see p66).

Method

The samples were soaked in a weak solution of hydrogen peroxide (H_2O_2), in order to disaggregate the sediment, and then wet sieved through a 500μm mesh. The residue retained was then soaked in further H_2O_2, and processed using the flotation technique (French 1971), with meshes of 500μm for both the flot and residue fractions. Flots of waterlogged samples were stored wet prior to analysis, while all other flots and all residues were air dried before detailed examination. An assessment was made of all the sample flots and coarser residue fractions, following which a selection was made of samples for more detailed analysis, all of which were medieval in date. These samples were examined for their plant macro remains content by Julie Jones, while palaeoentomological (insect) examination was also carried out on samples ◊9 and ◊10 by Dr David Smith.

Samples ◊1, ◊4, ◊7, ◊8 and ◊13 contained charred material, predominantly cereal grain, but also chaff, weed seeds and charcoal (Table 11). Many also contained fragments of burnt animal bone (see p43). Three further samples produced primarily waterlogged plant remains, although two of these (samples ◊9 and ◊10) also were fairly rich in charred material. Sample ◊6 produced a smaller assemblage of waterlogged macrofossils and only a single charred cereal grain. Plant remains from these features are shown in Table 12. Cereal grain and chaff determinations are based on Jacomet (1989) and plant nomenclature and habitat information follows Stace (1991).

A total of 7L (12.2kg) from sample ◊9 and 8L (10.2kg) from sample ◊10 were processed for palaeoentomological examination using paraffin flotation as outlined by Kenward *et al.* (1980). The resulting flots were then sorted for insect remains using a low powered binocular microscope. The insect fragments recovered, mainly Coleoptera (beetles) were identified by direct comparison to the Gorham and Girling insect collections at the Institute for Archaeology and Antiquity, the University of Birmingham. A full species list for the insects recovered is presented in Table 13. The nomenclature used follows that of Lucht (1987), while to give an aid to comparison each of the species present has been assigned an ecological code. This is displayed in the final column of Table 13, and follows standard codings developed by Kenward and Hall (1995).

Table 10: Summary of environmental samples

Sample (w)	Vol. (litres)	Context no.	Feature no.	Period	Detailed analysis
1	10	615	Pit 611	medieval	plant macro
2	20	622	Pit 621	Roman	-
3	10	801	Ditch 616	Roman	-
4	10	796	Pit 805	medieval	plant macro
5	20	648	Trench slot 647	Roman	-
6	10	877	Ditch 875 (waterlogged)	?medieval	plant macro
7	10	1021	Pit 1019	medieval	plant macro
8	10	1024	Pit 1019	medieval	plant macro
9	100	1072	Pit 1068 (waterlogged)	medieval	insect and plant macro
10	60	1092	Pit 1091 (waterlogged)	medieval	insect and plant macro
11	-	monoliths	?stream/pond	?medieval	-
12	5	1110	Drain 1109	medieval	-
13	10	1183	Pit 1184	medieval	plant macro

Results
Charred plant remains (Table 11)
Most of the cultivated plants recovered were from the staple crops of the medieval period: wheat, barley, oats and rye, with additional evidence for peas and beans. Preservation of remains in a charred state was variable, and while many cereal grains could be determined as wheat (*Triticum* sp), many were also in a poor condition, being distorted, and with pitted and abraded surfaces. Many were so heavily deformed that a high proportion of grains remain unidentifiable ('Cereal indet.'). This poor preservation is thought to be a result of the moisture content of the grain and the temperature of burning, rather than post-depositional disturbance. In contrast most of the chaff and weed seeds were in good condition, although many of the wheat rachis internodes were too fragmentary to determine which form was present.

Bread/club Wheat (*Triticum aestivum/compactum*) and Rivet/macaroni Wheat (*Triticum turgidum/durum*).
The assemblages from all the features are predominantly wheat with most of the well-preserved grains of the short rounded form characteristic of hexaploid (bread) wheats common in early medieval contexts. The grains appeared to fall into two groups, those greater than 5mm in length, and a smaller number of more slender, shorter grains between 3.5 and 4mm. The wheat rachis internodes point to the presence of both hexaploid (bread/club wheat) and tetraploid (rivet/macaroni wheat) forms as described by Moffett (1991).

Barley (*Hordeum* sp)
Remains of barley were less frequent than the wheat and preservation was poor. The grains were generally deformed or the surface had been lost, so it was not possible to characterise ear and row form. Only the occasional rachis fragment was present. While wheat is likely to have been the preferred food grain, barley sown as a spring grown crop could have been used as a supplement to wheat or made into ale. However, the idea of malting is not supported by evidence of sprouting on any of the grains.

Oat (*Avena* sp)
Oats were also traditionally cultivated as a spring crop and were sometimes planted with barley for use both as human food or animal fodder. Many of the oat grains in the samples were in poor condition, but the recovery of a single oat pedicel with a detachment scar at the top suggests the presence of the hexaploid, common cultivated oat (*Avena sativa* type). A few other pedicels showed the distinctive reverse scar of the 'sucker mouth' characteristic of the wild hexaploid oat (*Avena fatua*) (Moffett 1987). A single floret with its characteristic horseshoe-shaped scar also confirmed the presence of wild oats. These may have been growing as crop weeds, along with brome (*Bromus* sp), stinking chamomile (*Anthemis cotula*) and cleavers (*Galium aparine*) also found in these deposits.

Rye (*Secale cereale*)
Rye is only present in three of the pit fills and is likely to have formed a minor component of the crops present. It may have occurred, like the oats, as a crop weed, although it is known from documentary sources that rye was sometimes grown with wheat as a mixed crop of 'maslin'. Rye is a winter sown cereal and is tolerant of poor light soils, drought and temperature extremes. It will grow on sandy soils, which were available locally, where other crops would grow less well.

Legumes (*Lathyrus/Vicia/Pisum* and *Vicia faba*).
Legumes were present in most of the samples and were most abundant in sample 1. Their preservation in a charred form seems to be less common than cereals, as they are less likely to come into contact with fire during cooking preparations. Although preservation was variable, with many of the seeds in a fragmentary state and having lost the hilum necessary for identification to species, it was possible to place the legumes into a number of groups. Species identified include *Pisum sativum* (pea) and *Vicia faba* (celtic/horse bean), probably cultivated as field or garden crops, and forming an important part of the staple diet. A few examples of common vetch (*Vicia sativa*) may have been from the sub-species *Vicia sativa* subsp. *sativa* which was commonly cultivated for fodder. Other vetches identified include smooth tare (*Vicia tetrasperma*) and grass vetchling (*Lathyrus nissolia*). All legumes would have been valued for improving the soil by their nitrogen fixing abilities in helping to improve the soil and may have been grown as part of a crop rotation system.

Other food plants
Other possible food plants include a single apple pip (*Malus sylvestris/domestica*), hazel nut fragments (*Corylus avellana*) and sloe/blackthorn stone fragments (*Prunus spinosa*). The hazel nuts and sloes are likely to have been collected from local hedgerows or scrub, while the apple could have been crab apples collected wild or a garden cultivar.

Arable weeds
Many of the weeds recovered are common species of disturbed and arable ground. While today many would not be considered as crop weeds, they are commonly recovered in the archaeobotanical record in contexts associated with charred cereals. This suggests that they were growing with these crops or on field margins, perhaps in or adjacent to boundary ditches (which may have been wet), and have all been gathered at harvest. The presence of wild oat and brome has been mentioned already and these may have grown with other weeds such as knotgrass (*Polygonum aviculare*), orache (*Atriplex* spp), docks (*Rumex* spp), stinking chamomile and thorow-wax (*Bupleurum rotundifolium*). A further group recovered, which are more commonly thought of today as grassland species, includes clovers/medicks (*Trifolium/Medicago*), black medick (*Medicago lupulina*), ribwort plantain (*Plantago lanceolata*) and selfheal (*Prunella vulgaris*). These may have grown on the grassy field margins, occasionally invading the cornfields. Spike-rush (*Eleocharis palustris/uniglumis*), a plant of damp places, also frequently occurs in a charred form in association with crop remains and it has been suggested that some parts of fields used for crops may have been poorly drained or that marginal land was being utilised (Jones 1978). While many of the weeds present do not have strong preferences for soil types, there are a number of exceptions. Thorow-wax has a preference for calcareous soils, while stinking mayweed will grow on damp, heavier, more clayey soils. Many of the grassland plants recovered could represent pasture, with suitable land existing in much of the area around the settlement and the charred remains may represent burnt dung from grazing animals.

Table 11: Plant remains from non-waterlogged features
Lathyrus/Vicia/Pisum *groups: Identification was made to species based on size, preservation of hilum and in some species surface pattern. Poorly preserved legumes were placed into groups 1–5, based on size and called* **Lathyrus/Vicia** *or* **Lathyrus/Vicia/Pisum**, *but it is suggested that these may be the same species as those positively identified in that group.*

KEY TO HABITATS			
A:	Aquatic	a:	acidic
B:	Bankside	c:	calcareous
C:	Cultivated/Arable	d:	dry soils
D:	Disturbed	h:	heavy soils
E:	Heath/Moor	l:	light soils
G:	Grassland	n:	nitrogen rich soils
H:	Hedgerow	o:	open habitats
M:	Marsh	p:	phosphate rich soils
P:	Ponds, ditches, stagnant/slow-flowing water	s:	coastal
R:	Rivers, streams	w:	wet/damp soils
S:	Scrub	#:	cultivated plant/of economic importance
W:	Woodland		

Table 11: Plant remains from non-waterlogged features (continued)

	Context no.	615	796	1021	1024	1183	
	Sample no.	1	4	7	8	13	
	Sample size (litres)	10	10	10	10	10	
	Size of float (ml)	55	10	30	20	55	
	Common name						*Habitat*
GRAIN							
Triticum sp	Wheat	181	25	367	132	28	
cf. *Triticum* sp		57	9	146	30	14	
Triticum sp (small grains 3.5-4mm)		56	-	-	11	8	
Total:		294	34	513	173	50	
Hordeum sp	Barley	12	2	69	8	-	
cf. *Hordeum* sp		-	-	29	-	-	
Hordeum sp (tail grain)		11	-	4	-	-	
Total:		23	2	102	8	0	
Avena sp	Oat	18	7	33	7	15	
cf. *Avena* sp		-	-	12	3	11	
Total:		18	7	45	10	26	
Secale cereale	Rye	-	-	-	2	3	
Cereal indet		267	33	568	258	17	
Total:		602	76	1228	451	96	
CHAFF							
Triticum sp (free-threshing hexaploid rachis internode)	Bread Wheat	10	-	-	-	-	
Triticum sp (free-threshing tetraploid rachis internode)		-	-	2	-	-	
Triticum sp (tough rachis internode)	Wheat	103	-	3	-	-	
Triticum sp (rachis internode)		133	3	34	-	5	
Triticum sp (basal rachis internode)		9	-	-	-	-	
Triticum sp (rachis internode base)		2	-	-	-	-	
Triticum/Hordeum sp (awns - silicified)	Wheat/Barley	few	1	-	-	-	
Hordeum sp (rachis internode)	Barley	1	-	-	-	-	
Hordeum sp (rachis internode base)		-	1	-	-	-	
Avena sp (floret)	Oat	1	-	-	-	-	
Avena sp (pedicels - charred)		1	-	-	-	-	
Avena sp (pedicels - silicified)		1	-	-	-	-	
Avena sp (awns)		7	1	1	2	1	
Secale cereale (rachis internode)	Rye	-	-	-	-	2	
Cereal indet (culm nodes)		14	-	-	-	1	
Cereal indet (embryo area)		-	1	3	-	-	
Total:		282	7	43	2	9	
WEEDS							
Chenopodiaceae							
Atriplex spp	Orache	5	3	2		3	CDn
Polygonaceae							
Polygonum aviculare L.	Knotgrass	4	-	-	-	-	CD
Rumex spp	Dock	41	-	1	-	4	DG

Table 11: Plant remains from non-waterlogged features (continued)

Context no.	Common name	615	796	1021	1024	1183	Habitat
Sample no.		1	4	7	8	13	
WEEDS continued							
Rosaceae							
Prunus spinosa L. (nut frags)	Blackthorn	-	-	-	3	-	HSW
Rosaceae indet (thorn)		1	-	-	-	-	
Fabaceae							
Medicago lupulina L.	Black Medick	5	-	-	-	-	GR
Trifolium/Medicago spp	Clover/Medick	73	3	2	-	2	DG
Lathyrus/Vicia/Pisum groups	Pea/Vetch/Garden Pea						
1. *Vicia tetrasperma* (L.) Schreber (*c.* 1.5 x 1.5mm + hilum)	Smooth Tare	9	-	-	1	1	G
Lathyrus/Vicia spp (*c.*1.5 x 1.5mm no hilum) (+ halves)	Pea/Vetch	35 (12)	1 (1)	-	-	- (2)	
2. *Lathyrus nissolia* L. (2 x 2mm + hilum + surface pattern)	Grass Vetchling	1	-	-	-	-	G
L. cf. *nissolia* L. (2 x 2mm + surface pattern) (+ halves)	Grass Vetchling	3 (2)	-	-	-	-	G
Lathyrus/Vicia sp (2 x 2mm - 2.5 x 2.5mm, no hilum)	Pea/Vetch	15	-	-	-	-	
3. *Vicia sativa* L. (3 x 3mm + hilum)	Common Vetch	6	-	-	-	1	CDG#
Lathyrus/Vicia spp (3 x 3mm no hilum)	Pea/Vetch	44	-	-	-	-	
4. cf. *Pisum sativum* (4 x 4mm + ovate hilum)	Garden Pea	2	-	-	-	-	#
Lathyrus/Vicia/Pisum spp (4 x 4mm no hilum)	Pea/Vetch/Garden Pea	17	-	-	-	-	
Lathyrus/Vicia spp (4 x 4mm + narrow hilum)	Pea/Vetch	1	-	-	-	-	
5. *Lathyrus/Vicia/Pisum* sp (2-3 x 2-3mm: halves) (4-5 x 4-5mm: halves)	Pea/Vetch/Garden Pea	(13) (17)	- (4)	- -	- (6)	- -	
Vicia faba L.	Celtic/Horse Bean	2	-	-	-	-	#
cf. *Vicia faba* L. (halves only)		(9)	-	-	-	(1)	#
Apiaceae							
Apium graveolens L.	Wild Celery	1	-	-	-	-	ws
Conium maculatum L.	Hemlock	1	-	-	-	-	Bw
Plantaginaceae							
Plantago lanceolata L.	Ribwort Plantain	-	1	-	-	-	G
Plantago major L.	Greater Plantain	3	-	1	-	-	CDGo
Scrophulariaceae							
Odontites/Euphrasia spp	Bartsia/Eyebright	5	1	11	2	-	CD
Rubiaceae							
Galium aparine L.	Cleavers	3	-	-	-	-	CHSo
Caprifoliaceae							
Sambucus nigra L.	Elder	-	-	1	-	-	DHSWn

Table 11: *Plant remains from non-waterlogged features (continued)*

Context no.		615	796	1021	1024	1183	
Sample no.		1	4	7	8	13	
	Common name						Habitat
WEEDS continued							
Asteraceae							
Anthemis cotula L.	Stinking Chamomile	41	2	8	4	1	CDd
Anthemis cotula L. (receptacle with achenes attached)		-	-	-	-	1	CDd
Leucanthemum vulgare Lam	Ox-eye Daisy	-	-	2	-	-	G-rich soils
Cyperaceae							
Eleocharis palustris/uniglumis	Spike-rush	-	-	1	-	-	MPw
Poaceae							
Anisantha sterilis (L.) Nevski	Barren Brome	-	-	-	-	5	CD, G-open
Bromus spp	Brome	2	1	-	1	-	CD
Poa/Phleum spp	Meadowgrass/Cat's-tail	2	-	-	-	-	G
Poaceae indet (caryopsis)	Grass	4	-	-	-	9	G
Poaceae indet (culm nodes - silicified)		11	-	-	-	-	G
Indet		-	-	-	-	2	
Total:		337	12	29	11	29	
Charcoal (presence = *)		*	*	-	-	*	
Charcoal (fragments > 2mm) approx.		50	30	-	-	100	

Waterlogged plant remains (Table 12)

Three samples (◇6, ◇9 and ◇10) contained charred and waterlogged plant macrofossils and insect remains. Sample ◇9 was the primary fill of a wattle-lined pit (1068) and was highly organic, containing wood and leather fragments, and over 1800 well-preserved seeds, fruits and buds, as well as an assemblage of charred crop remains and a diverse insect fauna. Sample ◇10 was the primary fill from an intercutting pit (1091), and produced 1775 waterlogged plant remains. Sample ◇6 (a primary ditch fill) contained a more restricted assemblage of waterlogged remains and only a single wheat grain.

Many of the waterlogged weed seeds recovered from the fills of the two pits were of the same species as those recovered in a charred form. Arable weeds formed a large group, with oraches, docks, knotgrass and stinking mayweed the most abundant. Additional weeds not recovered in a charred form, but also typical of disturbed habitats, include common chickweed (*Stellaria media*), downy hemp-nettle (*Galeopsis segetum*) and narrow-fruited cornsalad (*Valerianella dentata*). Weeds normally regarded as more typical grassland species were preserved both charred and waterlogged.

Many of the arable weeds do not have specific ecological requirements apart from their adaptation to disturbed ground. Common chickweed, for example, commonly occurs on moist, well aerated soils in Britain today, but equally favours habitats such as waste places, farmyards and roadsides where there is continual or periodic soil disturbance (Sobey 1981). Small nettle (*Urtica urens*) and stinking chamomile both occur around farmyards and waste ground, but the former is abundant on arable land, particularly light soils, and the latter will not grow in undisturbed habitats (Kay 1971). Therefore while many of the segetals (weeds of crops) may have been gathered in at harvest, they could equally have grown on waste ground around the site with many of the species more commonly associated with human habitation. These include common nettle (*Urtica dioica*) and elder (*Sambucus nigra*), both found in large quantities. These plants occur in nutrient-rich ground around settlements, where continual trampling would have provided bare ground for weeds to flourish. Elder and blackberry (*Rubus* sect Glandulosus) are particularly abundant in sample ◇6, so it is suggested that this ditch may have run alongside an area of scrubby vegetation. Areas of scrub would also have provided a habitat for hazel and blackthorn, which could have been gathered as kindling for hearths or ovens as well as providing an additional food source. Wood charcoal was present throughout the features examined although was not identified to species. The large numbers of willow buds (*Salix* spp), many still attached to small twigs, as well as a few oak (*Quercus* sp) buds, however, suggest the utilisation of these two additional species. Oak, willow and hazel are all species suitable for coppicing.

A further group of plants recovered is more typical of wet places, such as damp marshy ground which may have been present not far away from the settlement or, as suggested previously, they may have invaded field margins from adjacent unploughed fields or boundary ditches. The basal fill of ditch 875 contained many achenes of celery-leaved buttercup (*Ranunculus sceleratus*), as well as seeds of hemlock (*Conium maculatum*), water plantain (*Alisma* sp) and sedges (*Carex* spp). This suggests that the ditch may have been at least seasonally wet, as celery-leaved buttercup is a characteristic plant of nutrient-rich, seasonally exposed mud or shallow water at the margins of ponds and rivers, and water plantain of shallow margins of streams and ponds (Haslam *et al.* 1975).

Table 12: Plant remains from waterlogged features
For notes and Key to Habitats see Table 11

Context no.		877	1072	1092	
Sample no.		6	9	10	
Sample size (litres)		10	20	20	
Size of float examine (ml)		150	530	480	
	Common name				Habitat
WATERLOGGED REMAINS					
Ranunculaceae					
Ranunculus acris/repens/bulbosus	Meadow/Creeping/Bulbous Buttercup	1	114	49	DG
Ranunculus flammula L.	Lesser Spearwort	-	1	-	MPRw
Ranunculus sceleratus L.	Celery-leaved Buttercup	191	2	1	MPR
Papaveraceae					
Papaver rhoeas/dubium/hybridum/lecoqii	Poppy	-	2	1	CD
Urticaceae					
Urtica dioica L.	Common nettle	216	7	46	DGHWp
Urtica urens L.	Small nettle	-	12	57	CDl
Fagaceae					
Quercus sp (twigs with bud)	Oak	-	-	2	HSW
Betulaceae					
Corylus avellana L. (nut frags)	Hazel	-	2	-	HSW
Chenopodiaceae					
Atriplex spp	Orache	-	136	558	CDn
Chenopodiaceae indet		-	7	-	

Table 12: Plant remains from waterlogged features (continued)

Context no.	Common name	877	1072	1092	Habitat
Sample no.		6	9	10	
WATERLOGGED REMAINS continued					
Caryophyllaceae					
Agrostemma githago L.	Corncockle	-	-	2+f	C
Cerastium sp	Chickweed	-	7	1	CDG
Stellaria media (L.) Villars	Common Chickweed	-	24	15	CD
Polygonaceae					
Fallopia convolvulus (L.) A. Love	Black-bindweed	-	1	7	CD
Persicaria maculosa Gray	Redshank	-	1	3	CDo
Polygonum aviculare L.	Knotgrass	-	25	280	CD
Rumex conglomeratus Murray	Clustered Dock	-	-	5	BGw
Rumex cf. *conglomeratus*		-	11	-	
Rumex spp	Dock	1	191	53	DG
Clusiaceae					
Hypericum spp	St. John's Wort	-	1	-	
Salicaceae					
Salix spp (buds)	Willow	-	50	57	w
Salix spp (small twigs with buds)		-	8	5	w
Brassicaceae					
Brassica/Sinapis/Raphanus spp	Mustard/Rape/Cole etc.	-	232	12	CD#
Raphanus raphanistrum ssp *Raphanistrum* (whole pods + seeds)	Wild Radish	-	14	-	CD
Raphanus raphanistrum ssp *Raphanistrum* (pod frags)		-	18	2	CD
Primulaceae					
Anagallis arvensis L.	Scarlet Pimpernel	-	25	12	CW
Primula veris/elatior	Cowslip/Oxlip	-	22	-	Gl/W
Rosaceae					
Aphanes arvensis L.	Parsley-piert	-	1	-	CGd
Filipendula ulmaria (L.) Maxim	Meadowsweet	-	1	-	w
Potentilla spp	Cinquefoil	-	1	-	EGa
Prunus domestica L.	Plum	-	2	-	HS#
Prunus spinosa L.	Blackthorn/Sloe	-	1	-	HSW
Rosaceae indet (thorn)		2	4	-	HSW
Rubus sect. *Glandulosus* Wimmer and Grab	Bramble	826+f	13	10	DHSW
Fabaceae					
Fabaceae indet (calyces)	Pea family	-	5	-	
Medicago lupulina L.	Black Medick	-	4	1	GR
Trifolium/Medicago sp (pod caps)	Clover	-	4	-	DG
Ulex sp (spine)	Gorse	4	-	-	EGWo
Euphorbiaceae					
Euphorbia cf. *exigua* L.	Dwarf Spurge	-	-	1	C
Linaceae					
Linum catharticum L.	Fairy Flax	-	4	-	G

Table 12: Plant remains from waterlogged features (continued)

Context no.		877	1072	1092	
Sample no.		6	9	10	
	Common name				Habitat
WATERLOGGED REMAINS continued					
Apiaceae					
Aethusa cynapium L.	Fool's Parsley	-	7	10	C
Apium graveolens L.	Wild Celery	-	1	-	ws
Bupleurum rotundifolium L.	Thorow-wax	-	2	4	C
Chaerophyllum aureum L.	Golden Chervil	-	43	17	G
Conium maculatum L.	Hemlock	2	5	95	Bw
Torilis spp	Hedge-parsley	-	15	19	
Solanaceae					
Hyoscyamus niger L.	Henbane	-	1	2	Bw
Solanum dulcamara L.	Bittersweet	10	-	-	DHS
Solanum nigrum L.	Black Nightshade	-	1	39	CD
Lamiaceae					
Galeopsis segetum Necker	Downy Hemp-nettle	-	4	11	CD
Galeopsis tetrahit L.	Common Hemp-nettle	-	1	-	CW
Mentha aquatica L.	Water Mint	-	1	-	MPw
Mentha spp	Mint	11	-	-	CDPW
Prunella vulgaris L.	Selfheal	-	28	4	DG
Satureja hortensis	Summer Savory	6	-	-	#
Stachys palustris L.	Marsh Woundwort	16	-	1	PRW
Plantaginaceae					
Plantago major L.	Greater Plantain	1	42	12	CDGo
Scrophulariaceae					
Odontites/Euphrasia spp	Bartsia/Eyebright	-	52	18	CD
Rhinanthus minor L.	Yellow Rattle	-	1	-	G
Caprifoliaceae					
Sambucus nigra L.	Elder	434+f	61	118	DHSWn
Valerianaceae					
Valerianella dentata (L.) Pollich	Narrow-fruited Cornsalad	-	3	6	CD
Dipsacaceae					
Dipsacus spp	Teasel	frags	1	-	DRW/?#
Asteraceae					
Anthemis cotula L.	Stinking Chamomile	-	286	123	CDh
Bellis perennis L.	Daisy	-	6	1	G
Carduus spp	Thistle	-	1	-	CDG
Centaurea cyanus L.	Cornflower	-	1	1	CD
Cirsium/Carduus spp	Thistle	1f	4	3	CDGH
Lapsana communis L.	Nipplewort	-	16	21	DH
Leontodon spp	Hawkbit	-	9	1	G
Leucanthemum vulgare Lam	Oxeye Daisy	-	4	3	G-rich soils
Picris echioides L.	Bristly Oxtongue	-	57	60	DHWc
Picris hieracioides L.	Hawkweed Oxtongue	-	9	4	DGoc
Senecio cf. *aquaticus* Hill	Marsh Ragwort	-	4	-	MPRw

Table 12: Plant remains from waterlogged features (continued)

Context no.		877	1072	1092	
Sample no.		6	9	10	
	Common name				Habitat
WATERLOGGED REMAINS continued					
Asteraceae continued					
Sonchus arvensis L.	Perennial Sow-thistle	-	11	4	CDPRs
Sonchus asper (L.) Hill	Prickly Sow-thistle	1	25	7	CD
Sonchus oleraceus L.	Smooth Sow-thistle	-	2	5	CDW
Alismataceae					
Alisma spp	Water Plantain	8	-	-	APR
Juncaceae					
Juncus spp	Rush	-	c. 100	-	GMRw
Cyperaceae					
Carex spp	Sedge	12	-	-	GM
Eleocharis palustris/uniglumis	Spike-rush	-	43	-	MPw
Poaceae					
Glyceria spp	Sweet-grass	-	20	-	MPRw
Poa/Phleum spp	Meadowgrass/Cat's-tail	-	-	1	G
Poaceae indet	Grass	2	37	-	DG
Indet		-	7	5	
Wood and twig fragments		-	abund	abund	
Total:		1739	1844	1775	
CHARRED REMAINS					
GRAIN					
Triticum sp	Wheat	1	66	98	
cf. *Triticum* sp		-	10	37	
Triticum sp (small grains 3.5-4mm)		-	3	9	
Total:		1	79	144	
Hordeum sp	Barley	-	11	16	
Hordeum sp (tail grain)		-	-	3	
Total:		0	11	19	
Avena sp	Oat	-	26	65	
cf. *Avena* sp		-	11	-	
Avena fatua (with floret + horseshoe shaped scar)	Wild oat	-	1	-	
Avena sp (with floret)	Oat	-	1	-	
Total:		0	39	65	
Secale cereale	Rye	-	-	2	
Cereal indet		-	23	67	
Total:		1	152	297	
CHAFF					
Triticum sp (free-threshing hexaploid rachis internode)	Bread Wheat	-	4	1	
Triticum sp (free-threshing tetraploid rachis internode)		-	-	5	
Triticum sp (tough rachis internode)	Wheat	-	9	14	
Triticum sp (rachis internode)		-	8	5	
Triticum sp (basal rachis internode)		-	1	-	
Triticum sp (rachis internode base)		-	-	3	

Table 12: Plant remains from waterlogged features (continued)

Context no. Sample no.	Common name	877 6	1072 9	1092 10	Habitat
CHAFF continued					
Triticum/Hordeum sp (awns)	Wheat/Barley	-	5	-	
Hordeum sp (rachis internode)	Barley	-	7	2	
Hordeum sp (rachis internode base)		-	6	-	
Hordeum sp (rachis internode with several segments)		-	1	-	
Avena fatua (pedicel)	Wild oat	-	3	-	
Avena sativa (pedicel)	Cultivated oat	-	1	-	
Avena sp (awns)		-	3	-	
Secale cereale (rachis internode)	Rye	-	2	-	
Cereal indet (culm nodes)		-	9	-	
Cereal indet (embryo area)		-	1	-	
Total:		-	60	30	
WEEDS					
Ranunculaceae					
Ranunculus acris/repens/bulbosus spp	Buttercup	-	1	-	DG
Fagaceae					
Quercus sp (bud)	Oak	-	1	-	HSW
Betulaceae					
Corylus avellana (nut frag)	Hazel	-	-	2f	HSW
Chenopodiaceae					
Atriplex spp	Orache	-	7	1	CDn
Polygonaceae					
Polygonum aviculare L.	Knotgrass	-	5	1	CD
Rumex sp	Dock	-	10	8	DG
Brassicaceae					
Raphanus raphanistrum ssp *raphanistrum* (pod frag)	Wild Radish	-	-	1	CD
Primulaceae					
Anagallis arvensis L. (cluster of seeds on flowerhead)	Scarlet Pimpernel	-	5	-	CW
Rosaceae					
Malus sylvestris/domestica	Crab Apple/Apple	-	-	1	HSW#
Fabaceae					
Medicago lupulina L.	Black Medick	-	1	3	GR
Trifolium/Medicago spp	Clover/Medick	-	48	30	DG
Lathyrus/Vicia/Pisum groups	Pea/Vetch/Garden Pea				
1. *Vicia tetrasperma* (L.) Schreber (c. 1.5 x 1.5mm + hilum)	Smooth Tare	-	4	2	G
Lathyrus/Vicia spp (c. 1.5 x 1.5mm, no hilum)	Pea/Vetch	-	16	7	
(+halves)		-	-	(2)	
2. *Lathyrus nissolia* L. (2 x 2mm + hilum + surface pattern)	Grass Vetchling	-	-	1	G
Lathyrus. cf. *nissolia* L. (2 x 2mm + surface pattern)		-	1	-	G
Lathyrus/Vicia spp (2 x 2mm - 2.5 x 2.5mm, no hilum)	Pea/Vetch	-	-	4	
3. *Lathyrus/Vicia* spp (3 x 3mm, no hilum)		-	8	-	

Table 12: Plant remains from waterlogged features (continued)

Context no.		877	1072	1092	
Sample no.		6	9	10	
	Common name				Habitat
WEEDS continued					
Lathyrus/Vicia/Pisum **groups** continued					
4. *Lathyrus/Vicia/Pisum* spp (4 x 4mm, no hilum)	Pea/Vetch/Garden Pea	-	1	4	
Vicia faba L.	Celtic/Horse Bean	-	-	1	#
Apiaceae					
Bupleurum rotundifolium L.	Thorow-wax	-	2	-	C
Torilis sp	Hedge-parsley	-	1	-	
Solanaceae					
Hyoscyamus niger L.	Henbane	-	2	-	Bw
Lamiaceae					
Prunella vulgaris L.	Selfheal	-	1	-	DG
Plantaginaceae					
Plantago lanceolata L.	Ribwort Plantain	-	1	-	G
Scrophulariaceae					
Odontites/Euphrasia spp	Bartsia/Eyebright	-	3	6	CD
Asteraceae					
Anthemis cotula L.	Stinking Chamomile	-	19	9	CDd
Anthemis sp. (receptacle)	Chamomile	-	-	1	
Picris echioides L.	Bristly Oxtongue	-	-	2	DHWc
Poaceae					
Anisantha sterilis (L.) Nevski	Barren Brome	-	-	3	CDGo
Bromus spp	Brome	-	3	1	CD
Poa/Phleum spp	Meadow-grass/Cat's-tail	-	6	1	G
Poaceae indet (caryopsis)	Grass	-	9	1	
Poaceae indet (culm nodes - charred)		-	3	-	
Total:		-	158	88	
Charcoal (presence = *)		-	*	*	
Charcoal (fragments > 2mm)		-	-	c. 100	

Entomological remains (Table 13)

Both waterlogged samples examined for their insect content produced relatively large and diverse faunas. The vast majority are the remains of beetles (Coleoptera). Also present in comparatively small numbers were the remains of adult flies (Diptera), ants (Formenicoidea), bugs (Hemiptera) and earwigs (Dermaptera). A few fly puparia were encountered but were not readily identifiable to species.

The vast majority of beetles recovered are commonly found living in and around human settlement. In particular many are associated with rotten and decaying organic waste, those species associated with decaying matter (ecological group RT) accounting for between 71% and 65% of the species present. Furthermore, it is clear that the material was particularly foul. Taxa such as the hydrophilids *Cercyon impressus*, *C. atricapillus* and the rove beetle *Platystethus arenarius* are commonly associated with well rotted material such as broken down stabling waste and thoroughly decayed domestic and farm rubbish. Two other species incorporated into this ecological grouping, the two dung beetles *Aphodius fimentarius* and *A. granaries*, are normally associated with the dung of large herbivores lying in open pasture. However, it is suspected that these species may well be capable of breeding in rotting vegetation around settlements (Jessop 1986, Kenward and Hall 1995).

In addition to these rather specialised species a wide range of insects indicative of mouldering and decaying organic matter in general occur, amongst them large numbers of rove beetles from the *Omalium, Oxytelus, Leptacinus, Neobisnus, Gabrius, Philonthus* genus, as well as *Coprophilus stiatulus*. Other species which live in mouldering and decaying plant and animal wastes are the other hydrophilids, the minute 'pill beetle' *Actritus nigricornis*, the scarabaedid *Oxymus silvestris* and the two *Anthicus* species; while *Trogophloeus bilineatus*, *T. fuliginosus* and *Platystethus nodifrons*, which are found today in muddy ground beside water courses (Tottenham 1954), may be from the same community. It has become clear from a range of archaeological studies that in the past these species were common in and around human settlement, probably in 'puddled' mud in yards and on floors (Hall *et al.* 1983, Hall and Kenward 1990, Kenward and Allison 1994, Kenward and Hall 1995, Smith *et al.* 1997). The importance of the above species can be seen from the fact that the general rotting matter ecological grouping (RT) accounts for 46% (sample ◇9) and 32% (sample ◇10) of the faunas.

Kenward recognises an association of species that are particularly representative of human habitation, and has labelled this fauna, perhaps misleadingly, as the 'house fauna' (Kenward and Hall 1995). Relatively few of these species were encountered at Stoke Road, accounting for between 7% and 15% of the overall fauna in samples ◇9 and ◇10 respectively. These species include *Xylodromus concinnus*, the cryptophagids and lathridiids, *Typhaea stercorea*, *Mycetaea hirta* and the 'spider beetle', *Tipnus unicolor*. All are associated with relatively dry matter and appear to have been common in cold and damp housing. However, only one individual of *Aglenus bruneus*, a species which in the past seems to have been typical of such domestic housing, was recovered (Hall *et al.* 1983, Hall and Kenward 1990, Kenward and Hall 1995). Two species of woodborers associated with prepared and aged timbers from domestic and settlement structures are present, the 'woodworm', *Anobium punctatum*, and the 'death watch beetle', *Xestobium rufovillosum*. Although normally associated with the smaller branches of a range of trees from woodland, the 'bark beetle' *Scolytus mulitstriatus* may also be found on new unseasoned 'barked' wood such as lathes and poles used in wattle work.

Only a small proportion of the species present appear to have been derived from outside the pits (represented by ecological grouping oa in Table 13). This includes a limited range of ground beetles that provide some indication of the nature of the environment directly adjacent to the pits. Species such as *Nebria salina*, *Loricera pilicornis*, *Clivina fossor*, *Pterostichus melanarius* and *Platynus dorsalis* are all typically inhabitants of disturbed, cultivated and sometimes muddy ground near to agricultural settlements (Lindroth 1974, Robinson 1979, Smith 1991). There are also some indications from the insects present of nearby pasture in the form of a range of plant feeding weevils such as *Sitona suturalis* and the *Rhinocus* species, which specifically feed on clover and dock respectively. However, if the material in the pits was derived from stabling or bedding material, these species may originally have come from cut fodder, such as meadow hay (Kenward and Hall 1997).

There are only two species present which suggest the presence of a nearby body of water, the small hydraenid, *Ochthebius minimus*, and the cyrsomelid, *Prasocuris phellandri*. *P. phellandri* feeds on various species of waterside Umbelliferae (= Apiaceae) (Koch 1992), while the small water beetle *O. minimus* is not limited solely to pond-sized bodies of water, but may also visit small temporary muddy puddles and pools (Hansen 1987).

Table 13: The insect remains from waterlogged features

> KEY TO ECOLOGIES (after Kenward and Hall 1995)
> oa: species which will not breed in human housing.
> w: aquatic species.
> d: species associated with damp watersides and river banks.
> rd: species primarily associated with drier organic matter.
> rf: species primarily associated with foul organic matter often dung.
> rt: insects associated with decaying organic matter but not belonging to either the rd or rf groups.
> l: species associated with timber.
> h: members of the 'house fauna' this is a very arbitrary group based on archaeological associations (Hall and Kenward 1990)

	Context no.	1072	1092	
	Sample no.	9	10	
				Ecology
COLEOPTERA				
Carabidae				
Nebria salina Fairm. Lab.		1	-	oa
Loricera pilicornis Latr.		1	-	oa
Clivina fossor (L.)		1	1	oa
T. quadristriatus (Schrk) *T. obtusus* Er.		1	-	oa
Trechoblemus micros (Hbst.)		-	1	oa
Bembidion aeneum Germ.		2	1	oa
B. guttula (F.)		-	1	oa
Bembidion sp.		-	1	oa
Pterostichus melanarius (Ill.)		1	1	oa
Platynus dorsalis (Pont.)		1	-	oa
Amara sp.		1	-	oa
Hydraenidae				
Hydraena sp.		1	-	oa-w
Ochthebius minimus (F.)		-	1	oa-w
O. spp.		-	1	oa-w
Helophorus spp.		1	-	oa-w
Hydrophilidae				
Cercyon impressus Sturm		7	4	rf
C. atricapillus (Marsh.)		7	3	rf
C. analis (Payk.)		-	7	rt
C. spp.		2	6	rt
Megasternum boletophagum (Marsh.)		1	2	rt
Histeridae				
Acritus nigricornis (Hoffm.)		1	3	rt
Silphidae				
Silpha spp.		1	-	-
Scydmaenidae				
Scydmaenidae spp. and Gen. indet.		1	-	-
Ptiliidae				
Ptilidae Genus and spp. indet.		3	-	rt

Table 13: The insect remains from waterlogged features (continued)

Context no. Sample no.	1072 9	1092 10	Ecology
COLEOPTERA continued			
Staphylinidae			
Micropeplus sp.	1	-	rt
Megarthrus sinuatocollis (Boisd. Lacord)	1	1	rt
Omalium rivulare (Payk.)	-	2	rt
O. caesum Grav.	-	1	rt
Omalium spp.	2	-	rt
Xylodromus concinnus (Marsh.)	3	1	rt-h
Coprophilus striatulus (F.)	-	1	rt
Trogophloeus bilineatus (Steph.)	7	4	rt
T. fuliginosus (Grav.)	2	-	-
T. spp.	4	6	-
Oxytelus sculptus Grav.	8	5	rt
Oxytelus rugosus (F.)	4	5	rt
O. nitidulus Grav.	5	4	rt-d
Platystethus arenarius (Fourc.)	13	13	rf
P. nodifrons (Man.)	1	-	oa-d
Stenus spp.	1	1	-
Leptacinus cf. batchrus (Gyll.)	1	3	rt
Gyrohypnus fracticornis (Müll.)	2	1	rt
Neobisnius spp.	1	1	rt
Gabrius spp.	-	1	rt
Philonthus spp.	2	1	-
Tachinus sp.	1	-	-
Tachyporus sp.	1	-	-
Falagria spp.	-	1	rt
Aleocharinidae Genus and spp. Indet.	7	6	-
Pselpahidae			
Trichonyx sulcicollis (Reichb.)	-	1	-
Bryaxis sp.	1	-	-
Nitidulidae			
Meligethes sp.	1	-	oa
Cryptophagidae			
Cryptophagus ?scanicus (L.)	1	-	rd-h
C. spp.	2	1	rd-h
Atomaria spp.	2	2	rd-h
Lathridiidae			
Enicmus minutus (Group)	4	2	rd-h
Corticaria/corticarina sp.	-	1	rt
Mycetophagidae			
Typhaea stercorea (L.)	2	-	rd
Colydiidae			
Aglenus brunneus (Gyll.)	1	-	rt-h
Endomychidae			
Mycetaea hirta (Marsh.)	1	1	rd-h

Table 13: The insect remains from waterlogged features (continued)

Context no.	1072	1092	
Sample no.	9	10	
			Ecology
COLEOPTERA continued			
Anobiidae			
Xestobium rufovillosum (Geer)	-	1	l
Anobium punctatum (Geer)	4	1	l
Ptinidae			
Tipnus unicolor (Pill. Mitt.)	4	1	rd-h
Anthicidae			
Anthicus formicarius (Goeze)	-	1	rt
Anthicus antherinus (L.)	1	2	oa
Scarabaeidae			
Oxymus silvestris (Scop.)	1	2	rt
A. fimentarius (L.)	1	-	oa-rf
A. granarius (L.)	1	2	oa-rf
Bruchidae			
Bruchus sp.	-	1	oa
Chyrsomelidae			
Prasocuris phellandri (L.)	1	-	oa-d
Phyllotreta spp.	1	1	oa
Scolytidae			
Scolytus multistriatus (Marsh.)	-	1	oa-l
Cuculionidae			
Apion spp.	3	1	oa
S. suturalis Steph.	2	-	oa
S. spp.	-	1	oa
Rhinocus spp.	-	1	oa
Ceutorhynchus sp.	1	-	oa
DIPTERA			
Diptera Family genus and spp. indet.	5+	5+	-
HYMENOPTERA			
Formicoidea Family Genus and spp. indet.	5+	5+	-

Discussion

Function and economy

The charred material is a mixture of products from the different stages of crop processing, most probably from crops grown in nearby fields, and the same may be the case for much of the waterlogged material, with additional evidence of plants growing in bare and disturbed ground around the settlement.

Samples with charred material are dominated by cereal grains, with wheat most common but, with the exception of sample ◇1 (from pit 611), crop-processing waste forms a minor element. The cereal chaff represents different stages in the processing of a cereal crop after harvesting, the commonly encountered chaff being removed at the winnowing stage. Coarse sieving would then remove the larger items such as culm nodes and larger weeds such as oats and brome. Many of the crop weeds present were small and would have been removed in the fine sieving towards the end of the process. As there is a mixture of grain, together with chaff and weeds from these different stages, it is likely that processing was carried out on the site. The presence of culm nodes from pit 611 indicates the presence of straw, confirming that the uncleaned crop was present.

Crop processing on the site may have included roasting grain to improve the flavour and make it easier to grind, although there is always the risk of charring the grain in the process. In a rural situation, people may also have ground their own grains at home for flour or have used a coarser meal in pottage, with crop-processing waste used as livestock fodder or as tinder in hearths and ovens, along with wood fuel. The charred fruits of sloe and apple, together with the wood charcoal, which was present in all samples, must also relate to fuel and probably represent the clearance of hearths and ovens. The varying quantities of charred cereal remains and chaff seen within the pits, together with the presence of charcoal, suggests that their fills represent the disposal of general domestic waste from a number of different sources, which of course may not have been the primary function of the pits.

The waterlogged plant remains from pits 1068 and 1091 (samples ◇9 and ◇10) also seem to represent rubbish disposal, with additional remains from vegetation growing locally around the site reflecting contemporary local conditions. These indicate a farmyard type environment with areas of bare ground where weeds could flourish, and neglected corners for nettles, elder and chickweed to thrive. It has been suggested that there were areas of scrub, particularly alongside ditch 875, which at times may have been water-filled.

The beetle evidence from pit 1068 provides further evidence for the disposal of a mixture of domestic and household rubbish, with many species present associated with rotten and decaying organic waste, although no remains of fly puparia, fleas or lice were found to help indicate the specific nature of this material. No evidence was forthcoming from the plant macrofossils to suggest the presence of cess, however the material in pit 1068 probably represents an accumulation of organic waste which had reached a fairly advanced stage of decay before or shortly after it had been placed into the pit.

Diet
Wheat is the dominant cereal at Stoke Road with both free-threshing hexaploid (bread wheat) and tetraploid (rivet/macaroni wheat) types present, but it was not possible to tell the relative importance of either crop. Bread wheat was until recently thought to be the most important wheat grown in medieval Britain, but with recent progress in the identification of rachis fragments there is increasing evidence for tetraploid wheats from excavations of medieval sites (Moffett 1991). These two groups of wheat have different bread-making qualities, bread wheat being the better as its high gluten content produces a lighter bread, while rivet wheat is a soft mealy grain perhaps more suitable for biscuit making (Percival 1921). It can also be mixed with bread wheat flour for baking.

Evidence of other cereals such as rye, oats and barley was sparse, although barley was more common from pit 1019 (sample ◇7). Barley may not have come into contact with fire if this crop was used as animal fodder, and this may be why it is less abundant than the wheat. Oats were often cultivated with barley as 'dredge' and could be used as fodder or food, although wild oats, also present, would have persisted as cornfield weeds. Rye seems to have been the least important cereal and could have been grown as part of a maslin crop with wheat.

Peas and beans are most likely to have been grown as field crops and may have either been for human consumption or, along with the other legumes, provided fodder. Used in soups and vegetable pottages, they would have provided much of the starch and protein in the daily diet (McLean 1981).

Other possible food plants include *Apium graveolens* (wild celery), an aromatic plant known as smallage, with culinary as well as medicinal uses (Dickson 1994, 62). The natural habitat of wild celery is salt-marshes; it is therefore unlikely to have been part of the local flora and must have been brought in from elsewhere (Stace 1991). *Satureja hortensis* (summer savory) and *Atriplex hortensis* (cf. garden orache) are leafy herbs, which were probably used as potherbs. Pit 1091 (sample ◊10) contained an abundance of *Atriplex* seeds although these were not identified to species. Potherbs were used in pottage, a kind of stew, often with the addition of aromatic herbs, which together with bread formed a substantial part of the diet. Many species of mint (*Mentha* spp) are common plants of damp ground and may have been collected wild, but could also have been cultivated as an aromatic potherb. Many of the distinctive fruits of wild radish (*Raphanus raphanistrum*) were also found, broken into single-seeded portions, some with the seeds still enclosed. McLean (1981) suggests wild radishes were gathered rather than grown and used for 'hotting up' pottages and sauces as well as a root vegetable. Other remains of fruits and nuts (hazel, sloe, apple), may be food gathered from local sources or represent the collection of firewood.

There is some evidence for the use of plants other than as a food source. This includes a few occurrences of teasel (*Dipsacus* spp) and gorse (*Ulex* spp). Fragmented fruits of teasel were found in pit 1068 and ditch 875 (sample ◊6), but it was not possible to tell whether fuller's teasel (*Dipsacus sativus*) or the wild teasel (*Dipsacus fullonum*) were present. Fuller's teasel would have been used in cloth manufacture in the final part of the process for raising the nap on the cloth by brushing, but wild teasel is a plant of rough ground, streams and woods, and the presence of teasel in ditch 875 makes it more likely that this is the species represented here. A few gorse (*Ulex* sp) spines were also found in the ditch fill. Gorse is a plant of heathland and is unlikely to have grown on the site, although it does grow on nearby Cleeve Hill at the present day. It may have been gathered for use as fuel and is known to have been used in bread ovens in the medieval period.

The Monolith Samples, by Keith Wilkinson and Nigel Cameron

Two monolith samples (sample ◊11) were taken through deposits within a depression at the southern end of the site during archaeological monitoring of the development groundworks subsequent to the main excavation. The purpose of sampling was to elucidate the origin of the depression, which was thought to represent a pond or a hollow, and to determine whether palaeoenvironmental analysis could inform on the past environment. The monolith tins were inserted into the 'pond' deposits and extracted to preserve an exact record of the sedimentary sequence.

Laboratory examination of the sampled sequence suggested that the deposits comprised re-worked Lias overlying a thin veneer of Cheltenham Sand. There was no evidence for the former presence of a pond. The re-working was probably indicative of erosion of the medieval surface and transport by overland flow to a low point. This was confirmed by diatom analysis of five monolith sub-samples, which demonstrated there was no sub-fossil preservation. This is extremely unusual in ponds, which generally have good biological preservation. Therefore it would appear that the depression at the southern end of the site was not a pond at all, but rather a hollow (perhaps resulting from stream action) that filled with sediment due to erosion of the contemporary ground surface, probably during the medieval period.

DISCUSSION

The results of the excavation indicate three principal phases of activity at Stoke Road, relating to the Roman, Saxon and medieval periods. The remains dating to the Roman period appear to represent the stock enclosures and funerary and metalworking areas of a relatively low-status Romano-British agricultural settlement of the 3rd to 4th century AD. Evidence for Saxon activity is limited to ephemeral structural remains, broadly dating to the 7th to 9th century. The medieval remains represent the rear yards and associated fields and enclosures of a series of tofts, dating to the 12th to 14th century. Like the earlier Romano-British and Saxon periods, the medieval features are indicative of settlement, but do not include evidence of actual dwellings. For the medieval period, it is assumed that the associated medieval houses stood at the southern end of the tofts, fronting onto Stoke Road.

Roman

Over the past few years a considerable amount of fieldwork has been undertaken in the Bishop's Cleeve area with occupation activity dating from the mid to late Iron Age through to the Saxon period being identified. Recently Barber and Walker (1998) and Parry (1999) have reviewed the growing evidence for Romano-British occupation within both the vicinity of Bishop's Cleeve and the wider context of this part of the Severn valley. They suggest that the Bishop's Cleeve evidence fits a wider pattern of sites indicative of a well-populated Romano-British landscape of small dispersed agricultural settlements. It is within this pattern of activity that the evidence from the Stoke Road excavations must be viewed.

The vast majority of the Romano-British pottery recovered dated to the 3rd and 4th centuries AD. A good proportion of this was Severn Valley ware with few tablewares or traded fabrics apparent, indicative of a fairly low-status settlement. Although a few sherds of residual 2nd-century pottery and later 4th-century Midlands shelly ware were found, along with a small coin hoard probably deposited in the period 340–50, it has not proved possible to chronologically differentiate phases of Roman activity.

The use of the Stoke Road site for agriculture and burial is likely to have been contemporary with Period 4 at Home Farm, which consisted of domestic activity adjacent to a stone building that lay to the south of the excavation area (Barber and Walker 1998). The lack of earlier features suggests that the Stoke Road evidence represents later expansion from an original focus of occupation centred near to the Cleeve Hall and Home Farm sites.

The Roman remains formed two distinct groups in the eastern half of the site. To the north, fields and enclosures were defined by ditches, generally aligned north-west/south-east. These were probably used as stock enclosures. Cattle appear to have been the main livestock and their mature age at death indicates they were primarily used as working animals before eventually being killed for meat. The significance of the two sheep buried in the area is unclear, but there was little evidence for pigs and none for domestic fowl: in all a fairly typical bone assemblage for a late Roman non-villa rural settlement.

To the south, a north/south-aligned boundary defined areas to the west and east. The earliest land-use to the west was as a small cemetery. Evidently the grave positions were not well marked as later Roman ditches cut across the area. Later ploughing had further damaged the burials, and further burials were probably completely lost. The remains of two males and two females (three adults, one juvenile) were identified, suggesting a family burial plot. A similar small group of burials has been identified at Gilder's Paddock (Parry 1999, 96–8); as with the Stoke Road burials, some graves were partly lined with stones, which may have supported unnailed coffins (Parry 1999). This practice is common in the region in graves of the later Roman period (Philpott 1991). The Gilder's Paddock burials are also in an area thought to be peripheral to the main settlement focus, an occurrence which Parry (1999, 101) has paralleled with Roughground Farm, Lechlade, where small groups of burials have been identified in several enclosures surrounding the villa but at some distance from it. Another small Romano-British burial plot set between enclosures has recently been excavated at Hucclecote (Bateman and Leah 1999, 16-18).

Although most of the eastern area lay beyond the edge of excavation, the large quantities of ironworking waste recovered from the various pits and ditches that formed the north/south boundary provided clear evidence of iron-smithing in the immediate vicinity. There was no evidence for iron-smelting, or for the use of coal (in contrast to the Home Farm site, where there was evidence for a coal-fuelled forge dating to the 2nd century). The use of scrap metal and poor quality welding suggests that ironworking was only being undertaken for the repair and fabrication of items for agricultural and domestic use. The small-scale industrial activity identified at Home Farm, which included horticulture and possibly tanning or flax-retting, appeared to have taken place within discrete zones inside enclosures (Barber and Walker 1998, 145-6).

The eastern area was subsequently the site for Structure 1, most of which again lay beyond the area of excavation. While the purpose of this structure was not established, the structural remains were clearly not those of the hypocausted masonry building, which was presumably sited nearby, judging by the quantities of Roman ceramic building material reused in a medieval cobbled surface. Recent work at Home Farm (Barber and Walker 1998; Hart 1992) and Cleeve Hall (Parry 1999, 101) has suggested the presence of a masonry building that may have formed the focus of settlement, although associated activity spread for some distance from this area.

Only a small area was uncovered at Stoke Road, but the Roman settlement appears to have been essentially agricultural, with stock enclosures and ditches arranged on the same alignment as those recorded at nearby Home Farm (Barber and Walker 1998). There was evidence for other activities such as the grinding of flour (fragments of millstone) and weaving (a spindlewhorl), as would be expected on a rural settlement of the later Roman period.

Saxon

The current evidence for early to middle Saxon activity in Bishop's Cleeve has recently been summarised in the discussion of the small 6th and 7th-century cemetery at Lower Farm, 1.5km to the west of Stoke Road (Holbrook 2000). The evidence recovered from Stoke Road, which comprises ephemeral structural remains, supports the growing evidence for post-Roman activity in the centre of Bishop's Cleeve. Seen within the context of the potential villa site located at Home Farm, Barber and Walker (1998) have suggested conformity with an emerging pattern from other sites, such as Frocester Court (Price 2000) and Barnsley Park (Webster *et al.* 1985), where land associated with a villa complex continued to be worked even though parts of the villa complex were no longer maintained.

Parry (1999) tentatively suggests that this possible continuity of settlement, coupled with the function of Cleeve Hall as an estate centre in the medieval period (see below), makes it tempting to identify Bishop's Cleeve as the focus of an estate centre continuously occupied during the Roman, Anglo-Saxon and medieval periods. Further work would be required to substantiate such a theory, given the limited nature of the activity identified at Stoke Road and given that the archaeological evidence suggests a hiatus in the settlement pattern between the late Saxon (9th century) and earliest medieval (12th century) deposits. However, the reuse at Stoke Road of Roman brick and tile in a 12th to 14th-century cobbled surface is significant in indicating the reuse and to some degree the survival of earlier buildings, albeit perhaps only as buried rubble.

Medieval, by Christopher Dyer

The first written evidence for Bishop's Cleeve shows that it was the site of a minster church (monastery) in the 8th century, which received royal patronage and was provided with a substantial landed estate (Aldred 1990, 22–23). In the 9th century the bishop of Worcester took control of the estate, and the minster diminished in importance. The parish church, as successor to the minster, remained a wealthy institution but the bulk of the revenues from its former lands went to the bishop. From the 11th century onwards the manor of Bishop's Cleeve, under the lordship of successive bishops of Worcester, contained the villages of Cleeve and Woodmancote, and part of Gotherington. Hamlets which have now disappeared lay on the slopes of the hill at Wick and at the eastern edge of the manor on top of Cleeve Hill at Wontley. The bishops of Worcester retained some rights of lordship over the surrounding villages, such as Brockhampton, Southam and Stoke Orchard, which in the 8th century had belonged to the Cleeve estate. These villages were also included within the extensive parish of Cleeve (Elrington 1968, 2–3).

At the centre of the bishop's manor lay a large and impressive house, which became the rectory after the Reformation and is now called Cleeve Hall. Parts of the present structure were built in the 13th century, and repairs in 1426–7 involved work on the solar and the steward's chamber (Elrington 1968, 20; WRO, ref. 009:1, BA 2636, 162/92116). A substantial part of a 15th-century manorial barn (now misnamed a tithe barn) stands nearby. Documents of the 14th century tell us that a complex of buildings, including a kiln, granary, pigsty and dovecote, was once associated with the bishop's manor house. There would also have been a stable and byre. The garden and orchard lay to the north-east, next to the churchyard (WRO, ref. 009:1, BA 2636, 193 92627, 12/12). Analysis of early maps suggests that the church, churchyard and original rectory occupied a rectangular block of land in the centre of the modern village, and the manor house and its many structures and enclosures lay immediately to the west. We can imagine that this division between parish church and manor dated from the bishop's take-over of the minster land in the 9th century.

Between the 11th and the 16th centuries, Cleeve was one of about twenty manors in the bishop's estate scattered over the west midland region. The bishop would have stayed occasionally for a few days or weeks at Cleeve during his travels through the diocese, as it was a convenient stopping place during regular progresses from Worcester to Bristol. The main purpose of the manorial complex was to provide the headquarters for the administration of the manor: here the steward would have stayed on his regular visits to hold the manor court. The receiver of the estate and other financial officials were accommodated in the manor house when touring the estate to collect money and to audit the accounts of the local reeve, who ran the manor from day to day. Above all, the manorial buildings provided the basis for the agricultural management of the demesne, which consisted at the end of the 13th century of 400 acres of arable and summer pasture for 1000 sheep (Hollings 1934–50, 327 & 349–50). In these buildings, animals were sheltered and equipment kept and maintained. The crops stored in barns and granaries were processed either for use on the manor (for the bishop's household, manorial servants and livestock), or for sale (Charles 1997, 27).

The Stoke Road site lay to the west of the manor house, and the structures of the 12th to 14th centuries as excavated may have included the fringes of the manorial site, but are likely to consist mainly of a row of peasant holdings that lay on the north side of Stoke Road. This row, together presumably with similar holdings on the south side of the road, which are shown on early maps, formed the westernmost extension of Cleeve village. This was created by the bishops by allocating parcels of demesne land adjoining their manorial centre. As the site lay so close to the manor house, the bishop's household could have been the source for some of the material recovered in the excavations, but much of the pottery, small finds and environmental evidence came from the peasant households located in the row of plots.

Little archaeological evidence had been recovered from medieval Bishop's Cleeve prior to the excavation at Stoke Road. Medieval property ditches were recorded at Gilder's Paddock (Parry 1999), further ditches were identified at the Junior School site (Isaac 1987) and east/west-aligned gullies, dated by pottery to the 12th to 14th centuries, were found at Home Farm (Barber and Walker 1998).

The archaeological remains encountered at Stoke Road comprised the rear yards of a series of tofts (Plots A to D), a building (Structure 4: possibly a barn, stable or shed) and associated enclosures or fields. Although a good deal of recutting of ditches and pits had clearly taken place, there was no evidence to indicate that any reorganisation of boundaries or areas of land-use had taken place whilst the site was in occupation. Virtually all of the pottery recovered dated the medieval activity to the 12th to 14th centuries.

Evidence for the medieval economy was gained from both animal bones and from palaeoenvironmental samples recovered from two waterlogged pits close to Structure 4. In contrast to the Romano-British period, sheep were the most commonly represented in the faunal bone assemblage, although generally of smaller stock than their Romano-British predecessors. Most bones were from adults, and were probably exploited mainly for their wool. Pig, horse, dog and cattle were also noted, the latter probably used as working animals. A wide range of species was recovered, including deer, chicken and goose, but only in relatively small quantities.

The palaeoenvironmental evidence is of particular interest as it is the largest assemblage recovered to date from a medieval site in Gloucestershire, and includes diverse flora and insect fauna. The staple crop was wheat, with barley, oats, rye, peas and beans also in evidence. The charred plant remains, along with two quern fragments, indicate that various stages of crop processing were undertaken at the site. Hazelnut, apple and sloes may have been used as fuel for hearths and ovens as well as for food. Wood charcoal was identified as willow and oak, both of which were suitable for coppicing.

The apparent abundance of weeds suggests that areas of grassland lay in the immediate vicinity, perhaps confirming a pastoral use for field H to the rear of the tofts. The insect remains suggest that the waterlogged pits were located in a farmyard and that stabling waste, or thoroughly decayed domestic and farm rubbish, had been used to backfill the pits once they had lost their primary function (the original function for many of the pits located across the site is unknown). Other activities identified include occasional cobbling, and small-scale metalworking, probably related to the repair of domestic and agricultural tools.

The rich documentation from Cleeve in the late 14th century allows some comparison between the archaeological and written evidence for crops and animals. The types of grain recorded as being grown in the vicinity of the Stoke Road site are analysed in Table 14.

The environmental evidence accumulated on the site over a longer period, which explains some of the differences between the physical remains and the documentary evidence. Rye, for example, may have been grown in the 12th or 13th centuries but had disappeared by the late 14th. The documents show the crops produced, while the material evidence reflects consumption of grain and straw, which may explain the prominence of wheat in the surviving botanical remains. Barley, especially in grain originating from peasant households, might be expected to have figured in greater quantity in the botanical samples, as it is prominent in the tithe receipts, which were derived mainly from peasant crops. The documents refer to nettles and thistles, which also figure in the material remains, but we know in addition that vines, garlic, leeks, hemp and flax were cultivated in Cleeve. The written evidence warns us from assuming that finds recovered from a site necessarily came from the immediate vicinity. Much of the hay fed to Cleeve animals came from a meadow at Bredon in Worcestershire, another bishopric manor 10km from the site. Building timber on occasion was brought more than 30km from north Worcestershire, where large trees were relatively plentiful.

Table 14: Percentages of crops grown in Bishop's Cleeve in the late 14th century.
  The bishop's demesne figures are for sown acreage, the others for grain brought into the barn (Dyer 1980, 124; CCC, B14/2/3/6). *: a mixture of barley and oats

Land recorded (date)	Wheat	Barley/dredge*	Peas/beans	Oats	Total
Bishop's demesne (1372-95)	35	29	31	5	100
Rectory demesne (1396-7)	37	48	15	0	100
Tithe corn (1396-7)	36	55	8	1	100

The manorial accounts demonstrate the prominence of sheep among the livestock. At the end of September 1394 the bishop's flock numbered 610, though in addition there were 4 horses, 20 cattle, 119 pigs, 30 geese and 79 hens and capons (WRO, ref 009:1, BA 2636, 193/92627 12/12). The peasants also kept many sheep (when their small individual flocks are added together), which is reflected in the tithe of 134 new lambs collected by the rector in 1389–90; this means that 1340 lambs were born in the whole parish, and implies a total flock of more than 3000 sheep. In the same year 370 piglets were born, and among the domestic birds hatched were 300 geese and more than 1000 doves (CCC, B/14/2/3/1). Some of the meat consumed at Cleeve probably came from a distance, notably the venison, which may have been brought from one of the bishop's parks such as that at Blockley (some 22km away), or may have been a gift from a neighbour, such as Winchcombe Abbey.

Sheep bones rarely outnumber cattle bones found on archaeological sites of the medieval period (Albarella 1999), yet at Stoke Road sheep predominate during this period. Comparable evidence was found at the deserted medieval village at Upton in Gloucestershire (Hilton and Rahtz 1966). In this respect the archaeology provides support for the documentary evidence, however, pig was not well represented among the faunal assemblage despite being numerous among the livestock of the peasants and the lord.

Perhaps surprisingly, the pottery assemblage retrieved from the tofts comprises fine tablewares from a wide range of sources, including Gloucester, Bristol and North Wiltshire to the south, Winchcombe, Herefordshire and Worcestershire to the north, and Oxfordshire/Buckinghamshire to the east. This range of pottery suggests an establishment of rather higher status, and could be interpreted as rubbish from the bishop's manor. It is also noteworthy that a drain around the agricultural building reused roof slates that originally adorned a substantial building. As the site lay adjacent to the residence of a wealthy lord, the transfer and reuse of high-status materials is not surprising. Documentary evidence shows that stone slates were used on buildings in the bishop's manorial complex, for example on a kiln built in 1372–3 (WRO ref. 009:1, BA 2636, 161/92113 5/6).

The development and abandonment of the Stoke Road site mirrors the general changes in society in England as a whole and specifically in the village of Bishop's Cleeve. The rising population in the 12th century is reflected by the growth in the number of tenants in the bishop's manor, where 43 (including 8 slaves) are recorded in Domesday Book in 1086, and 83 in the survey of *c.* 1170 (Moore 1982; Hollings 1934–50, 350–3). Growth continued up to more than a hundred in 1299. Many of the new families established in this period were smallholders, who received their holdings from the bishops as lords of the manor. The bishops were pursuing a concerted policy of replacing slaves with tenants, which increased both rent income and the labour supply for the demesne. In 1086 there had been 19 bordars and 8 slaves. The bordars were tenants who did not have enough land to feed their families, and expected to gain some income by working for the lord or for their wealthier neighbours. The slaves had either no land, or small plots on very insecure terms, and worked full-time on the lord's demesne. By *c.* 1170, 35 smallholders were recorded instead of the 27 smallholders and dependants of 1086. Some were called bordars, but the others were listed under the headings of bracmen, cottars, oxmen, or simply as specialist workers. In the intervening century the slaves had been granted plots of land, and had become tenants of smallholdings, and a number of new tenants had been recruited. In all more than a dozen grants of house plots had been made, each with three to six acres in strips scattered over the village fields. The land probably came from the demesne, and these are the most likely circumstances in which the excavated plots in Stoke Road originated.

The location of the Stoke Road holdings next to the manor house suggests that the smallholders were expected to work for the lord. The detailed 1299 survey tells us more (Hollings 1934-50, 327-45). There were then a group of cotlands, stated in 1299 each to have twelve acres of land, though in a puzzling anomaly subsequent documents state that they each held six acres; perhaps the twelve-acre holdings were measured in small field acres, which were equivalent to six statute acres. In addition, fifteen tenants had three acres each, known as 'mondaymen' because they were obliged to do a day's labour service on the demesne each Monday. With only three acres on which to live, they would have returned to the demesne on other days to work for wages. The cotland holders, assuming that they had six statute acres, would have needed to find some paid work, but would not have been so hard pressed. The Stoke Road plots could have been attached to cotlands because the 1299 survey reveals that many of them were 'enchelonds', a local word for a type of tenancy found throughout England (Postan 1954). They held their lands for the usual mixture of labour service (two days each week for a cotland) and payments in cash. If the lord chose they would be exempted from all other obligations, but could be required to work for the lord full time, doing jobs which involved daily attendance, as cowherd, ploughman, woodward or gardener. The mondaymen do not seem to have been committed to such arduous and continuous tasks as a condition of tenancy, but they could still be hired to do full time jobs for pay (a combination of cash and grain) and this is implied by the surnames of two of the mondaymen in 1299: daya (dairymaid) and swineherd. Individuals among the cotland holders and the mondaymen could have ventured into a more independent living by taking work by the day, or by taking up a craft, like John Sutor (shoemaker), who was a mondayman in 1299.

We know that different types of tenant were distributed unequally between the different settlements in Bishop's Cleeve. The more substantial tenants with yardlands and half-yardlands, who did not seek to work for others but lived mainly on the produce of their land, were located to the east, up the hill, either 'above the town' in the higher parts of Cleeve, or at Woodmancote and Wontley. Some cotland holders lived in Woodmancote and on the east side of Cleeve also, but a number of them were located in Cleeve village. Most of the mondaymen were also living in Cleeve. The likely occupants of the excavated plots in Stoke Road therefore were either cotlanders with 'enchelond' duties, or mondaymen who were contracted by the year to work on the demesne.

The lot of the smallholders around 1300 was not a happy one. The monetary rewards of wage work were very low, and the price of basic foods high. The labour market was glutted with large numbers of workers, and grain production could not keep pace with the demand, especially in poor harvest years when yields were reduced by bad weather (Dyer 1998, 110–18). Their low standard of living may be reflected in the meagre evidence for structures on the Stoke Road site. When the Black Death struck in 1349 at least a third of the population of Cleeve died, judging from the lack of tenants a few months later (Dyer 1980, 238). In the long term Cleeve's tenants were halved in number, from 102 before the plague to 53 in the 1470s (WRO, ref 009:1 BA 2636, 161/92113 2/6). Even within a generation or two after 1349 the smallholdings were clearly the first to be relinquished by their tenants. They were associated with poverty, and with dependence on the lord. A few were completely abandoned, but more were amalgamated with other holdings so that a tenant with two or three cotlands or mondaylands could make a decent living. When a composite holding was created, the tenants naturally needed only one house or set of farm buildings, and he or she allowed buildings to fall into ruin. The clerk who compiled the bishop's manorial account in 1393–4 recorded a holding with standing buildings as a messuage ('a messuage and a cotland') but if the buildings had decayed the word 'toft' was used ('a toft and a mondayland': WRO, ref. 009:1, BA 2636, 193/92627 12/12). Four of the thirteen cotlands listed in the part of the account recording short-term leases were associated with messuages, and the rest with tofts. In the case of the mondaylands, six of the eight tenements were called tofts. This is of course the time when the sequence of pottery on the site comes to a virtual stop: the Stoke Road site had been abandoned.

The Stoke Road settlement was brought into existence in the 12th century when the lord secured a supply of workers, both those doing labour services and those hired for pay, for his demesne. The demesne was managed directly by the lord's officials in the 13th and 14th centuries, and the settlement was fully occupied by estate workers. The settlement decayed when the population declined, giving the tenants who survived a choice of acquiring more land and moving away from dependence on the lord. In about 1400, the bishops gave up direct management of agriculture, partly because of the high cost and scarcity of labour, and the demesne was leased to a farmer. These changes could be seen in the context of death and decline, but another dimension was the choice exercised by the tenants, and the greater freedom and prosperity that they enjoyed.

BIBLIOGRAPHY

WRO: Worcestershire Record Office
CCC: Corpus Christi College, Oxford

Albarella, U. 1999 '"The mystery of husbandry": medieval animals and the problem of integrating historical and archaeological evidence', *Antiquity* **73**, (282), 867–76
Albarella, U. and Davis, S. 1996 'Mammals and birds from Launceston Castle, Cornwall: decline in status and the rise in agriculture', *Circaea* **12**, 1–156
Aldred, D. 1990 *Cleeve Hill. The History of the Common and its People* Stroud, Alan Sutton
Barber, A. 1996 *Land off Stoke Road, Bishop's Cleeve, Gloucestershire: Archaeological Assessment* unpublished Cotswold Archaeological Trust Report **96400**
Barber, A.J. and Walker, G.T. 1998 'Home Farm, Bishop's Cleeve: Excavation of a Romano-British occupation site 1993–4', *Trans Bristol Gloucestershire Archaeol Soc* **116**, 117–40
Barton, K. 1963 'A medieval pottery kiln at Ham Green, Bristol', *Trans Bristol Gloucestershire Archaeol Soc* **82**, 95–127
Bass, W.M. 1987 *Human Osteology: A Laboratory and Field Manual* Missouri, Missouri Archaeological Society
Bateman, C. and Leah, M. 1999 'Prehistoric and Roman remains on the line of the Gloucester Business Park Link Road, Hucclecote. Excavations in 1998', *Glevensis* **32**, 15–18
Bevan, L. 1998 'Querns, millstones and rubbers', in P. Leach, 109
Biddle, M. 1990 *Object and Economy in Medieval Winchester (Artefacts from Medieval Winchester)* Winchester Studies **7/2**, Oxford, Oxford University Press
Blockley, K., Blockley, M., Blockley, P., Frere, S.S. and Stow, S. 1995 *Excavations in the Marlowe Car Park and surrounding areas. Part II: The finds* The Archaeology of Canterbury **V**, Canterbury, Canterbury Archaeological Trust
Booth, P.M. and Green, S. 1989 'The nature and distribution of certain pink grog-tempered vessels', *J Roman Pottery Stud* **2**, 77–84
Brothwell, D.R. 1972 *Digging up Bones* London, British Museum (Natural History)
Charles, F.W.B. 1997 *The Great Barn of Bredon. Its Fire and Rebuilding* Oxbow Monograph **76**, Oxford, Oxbow Books
Clark, J. (ed.) 1995 *The Medieval Horse and its Equipment* London, HMSO
Cunliffe, B.W. (ed.) 1968 *Fifth Report on the Excavations of the Roman fort at Richborough, Kent* Reports of the Research Committee of the Society of Antiquaries of London **XXIII**, London, Society of Antiquaries
Dickson, C. 1994 'Macroscopic fossils of garden plants from British Roman and medieval deposits', in D. Moe *et al.* (eds), 47–72
Driesch, A. von den 1976 *A Guide to the Measurement of Animal Bones from Archaeological Sites* Peabody Museum Bulletin **1**, Harvard, Harvard University
Dunning, G.C. 1968 'The stone mortars', in B.W. Cunliffe (ed.), 110–4
Dyer, C. 1980 *Lords and Peasants in a Changing Society. The Estates of the Bishopric of Worcester, 680–1540* Cambridge, Cambridge University Press
Dyer, C.C. 1998 *Standards of Living in the Later Middle Ages: Social Change in England c. 1200-1520* revised edition, Cambridge, Cambridge University Press
Egan, J. and Pritchard, F. 1991 *Dress Accessories* London, HMSO

Ellis, P. 1986 'Excavations in Winchcombe, Gloucestershire, 1962-1972; a report on excavation and fieldwork by B.K. Davison and J. Hinchcliffe at Cowl Lane and Back Lane', *Trans Bristol Gloucestershire Archaeol Soc* **104**, 95-138

Elrington, C.R. (ed.) 1968 *The Victoria County History of Gloucestershire* **8** Oxford, Oxford University Press for Institute of Historical Research

Farwell, D.E. and Molleson, T.I. 1993 *Poundbury Volume 2: The Cemeteries* Dorset Natur. Hist. Archaeol. Soc. Monograph **11**, Dorchester, Dorset Natural History and Archaeological Society

French, D.H. 1971 'An experiment in water sieving', *Anatolian Stud* **21**, 59-64

Garrard, I.P. 1995 'Other objects of copper alloy and silver', in K. Blockley *et al.*, 1061

Gracie, H.S. and Price, E.G. 1979 'Frocester Court Roman Villa. Second report 1968-77: The courtyard', *Trans Bristol Gloucestershire Archaeol Soc* **97**, 9-64

Grant, A. 1982 'The use of tooth wear as a guide to the age of domestic ungulates', in B. Wilson *et al.*, 91-108

Gray, H. 1977 *Anatomy* New York, Bounty Books

Grigson, C. 1982 'Sex and age determination of some bones and teeth of domestic cattle: a review of the literature', in B. Wilson *et al.*, 7-24

Gutierrez, A. and Roe, F. 1998 'Stone objects: mortars, discs, querns, whetstones and chopping boards', in J.R. Timby, 176-9

Hall, A.R. and Kenward, H.K. 1990 *Environmental evidence from the Colonia* The Archaeology of York **14/6**, London, Council for British Archaeology

Hall, A.R. and Kenward H.K. (eds) 1994 *Urban-rural Connexions: Perspectives from Environmental Archaeology* Symposia of the Association for Environmental Archaeology **12**, Oxford, Oxbow Books

Hall, A.R., Kenward, H.K., Williams, D. and Greig, J.R.A. 1983 *Environment and Living Conditions at Two Anglo-Scandinavian Sites* The Archaeology of York **14/4**, London, Council for British Archaeology

Hansen, M. 1987 'The Hydrophiloidea (Coleoptera) of Fennoscandia and Denmark', *Fauna Entomologica Scandinavica* **18**, Copenhagen, Scandinavian Science Press

Hart, P. 1992 *Hitchens Phases 10 and 11, Bishop's Cleeve: Archaeological Evaluation* unpublished Gloucestershire County Council Archaeology Section Report

Haslam, S.M., Sinker, C.A. and Wolseley, P.A. 1975 *British Water Plants* Field Studies 4, Shrewsbury, Field Studies Council Publications

Heighway, C. 1983 *The East and North Gates of Gloucester and associates sites. Excavations 1974-81* Western Archaeological Trust Excavation Monograph Series 4, Gloucester, Alan Sutton

Hilton, R.H. and Rahtz, P.A. 1966 'Upton, Gloucestershire, 1959-1964', *Trans Bristol Gloucestershire Archaeol Soc* **85**, 70-147

Holbrook, N. (ed.) 1998 *Cirencester: The Roman Town Defences, Public Buildings and Shops* Cirencester Excavations **V**, Cirencester, Cotswold Archaeological Trust

Holbrook, N. 2000 'The Anglo-Saxon cemetery at Lower Farm, Bishop's Cleeve: Excavations directed by Kenneth Brown, 1969', *Trans Bristol Gloucestershire Archaeol Soc* **118**, 61-92

Holbrook, N. and Bidwell, P.T. 1991 *Roman Finds from Exeter* Exeter Archaeological Report 4, Exeter, Exeter City Council

Hollings, M. 1934-50 *The Red Book of Worcester* Worcester, Worcestershire Historical Society (4 parts)

Hurst, D. 1992 'Pottery', in S. Woodiwiss (ed.), 132-54

Hurst, D. and Rees, H. 1992 'Pottery fabrics: a multi-periods series for the County of Hereford and Worcester', in S. Woodiwiss (ed.), 200-9

Isaac, J. 1987 'Junior School, Bishop's Cleeve', in B. Rawes (ed.) Archaeological Review 11, *Trans Bristol Gloucestershire Archaeol Soc* **105**, 245

Iscan, M.Y., Loth, S.R. and Wright, R.K. 1984 'Age estimation from the ribs by phase analysis: White males', *J Forensic Sci* **29**, 1094–1104

Jacomet, S. 1989 *Prahistorische Getreidefunde: a guide to the identification of prehistoric barley and wheat finds* Basel, Botanical Institute of the University, Department of Taxonomy and Geobotany

Jessop, L. 1986 *Dung Beetles and Chafers. Coleoptera: Scarabaeoidea* Handbooks for the Identification of British Insects **V/11**, London, Royal Entomological Society of London

Jones, M. 1978 'The plant remains', in M. Parrington (ed.), 93–110

Kay, Q.O.N. 1971 'Anthemis cotula', *J Ecol* **59**, 623–36

Keen, L. 1986 'Late Anglo-Saxon strap-ends of Dorset', *Proc Dorset Natur Hist Archaeol Soc* **108**, 195–6

Kenward, H.K. and Allison E.P. 1994 'A preliminary view of the insect assemblages from the Early Christian rath site at Deer Park Farms, Northern Ireland', in J. Rackham (ed.), 89–103

Kenward, H.K., Hall A.R. and Jones A.K.G. 1980 'A tested set of techniques for the extraction of plant and animal macrofossils from waterlogged archaeological deposits', *Scientific Archaeol* **22**, 3–15

Kenward, H.K. and Hall, A.R. 1995 *Biological evidence from Anglo-Scandinavian deposits at 16–22 Coppergate* The Archaeology of York **14/7**, London, Council for British Archaeology

Kenward, H.K. and Hall, A.R. 1997 'Enhancing bio-archaeological interpretation using indicator groups: stable manure as a paradigm', *J Archaeol Sci* **24**, 663–73

Koch, K. 1992 *Okologie* Die Kafer Mitteleuropas 3, Krefeld, Goecke & Evers

Lambrick, G. and Robinson, M.A. (eds) 1979 *Iron Age and Roman Riverside Settlements at Farmoor, Oxfordshire* CBA Research Report **32**, London, Council for British Archaeology

Langton, B., Ings, M., Walker, G. and Oakey, N. 2000 'Medieval field systems at Tinker's Close, Moreton-in-Marsh, Gloucestershire. Excavations in 1995–6', in N. Oakey (ed.), 15–23

Leach, P. 1982 *Ilchester Volume I: Excavations 1974–1975* Western Archaeological Trust Excavation Monograph Series **3**, Gloucester, Alan Sutton

Leach, P. 1998 *Great Witcombe Roman Villa, Gloucestershire: A Report on Excavations by Ernest Greenfield 1960–1973* BAR British Series **266**, Oxford, British Archaeological Reports

Leech, R. 1986 'The excavations of a Romano-Celtic temple and a later cemetery on Lamyatt Beacon, Somerset', *Britannia* **17**, 259–328

Lindroth, C.H. 1974 *Coleoptera: Carabidae* Handbooks for the Identification of British Insects **IV/2**, London, Royal Entomological Society of London

Lucht, W.H. 1987 *Katalog* Die Kafer Mitteleuropas, Krefeld, Goecke & Evers

Maltby, M. 1979 *Faunal Studies and Urban Sites: the Animal Bones from Exeter 1971–1975* Sheffield, University of Sheffield Department of Prehistory and Archaeology

Maltby, M. 1983 'The animal bones', in C. Heighway, 228–45

Maltby, M. 1994 'The meat supply in Roman Dorchester and Winchester', in A.R. Hall and H.K. Kenward (eds), 85–102

Maltby, M. 1997 'Domestic fowl on Romano-British sites: inter-site comparisons of abundance', *Int J Osteoarch* **7**, 402–14

Maltby, M. 1998 'Animal bones from Romano-British deposits in Cirencester', in N. Holbrook (ed.), 352–69

Manning, W.H. 1985 *Catalogue of the Romano-British Iron Tools, Fittings and Weapons in the British Museum* London, British Museum

McLean, T. 1981 *Medieval English Gardens* London, Collins

McMinn, R.M.H. and Hutchings, R.T. 1985 *A Colour Atlas of Human Anatomy* London, Wolfe Medical Publications

McWhirr, A., Viner, L. and Wells, C. 1982 *Romano-British Cemeteries at Cirencester* Cirencester Excavations **II**, Cirencester, Cirencester Excavation Committee

Mellor, M. 1994 'Oxfordshire pottery', *Oxoniensia* **LIX**, 17–217

Moe, D., Dickson, J.H. and Jorgensen P.M. 1994 *Garden History: Garden plants, species, forms and varieties from Pompeii to 1800* Ravello, Pact 42

Moffett, L. 1987 *The Macro-botanical Evidence from Late Saxon and Early Medieval Stafford* Ancient Monuments Laboratory Report **169/87**, London, English Heritage

Moffett, L. 1991 *The Archaeobotanical Evidence for Free-threshing Tetraploid Wheat in Britain* Palaeoethnobotany and Archaeology. International Work-group for Palaeoethnobotany. 8th Symposium, Nitra-Nove Vozokany, 1989, Nitra, Archaeological Academy of Sciences

Molleson, T.I. 1993 'The human remains', in D.E. Farwell and T.I. Molleson, 142–214

Moore, J. (ed.) 1982 *Domesday Book No. 15: Gloucestershire* Chichester, Phillimore

Mudd, A., Williams, R.J. and Lupton, A. 1999 *Excavations Alongside Roman Ermin Street, Gloucestershire and Wiltshire: The Archaeology of the A419/417 Swindon to Gloucester Road Scheme. Vol 2: Medieval and Post-medieval Activity, Finds and Environmental Evidence* Oxford, Oxford Archaeological Unit

O'Connor, T.P. 1991 *Bones from 46–54 Fishergate* The Archaeology of York **15/4**, London, Council for British Archaeology

Oakey, N. (ed.) 2000 *Three Medieval Sites in Gloucestershire* Cotswold Archaeological Trust Occasional Paper No. **1**, Cirencester, Cotswold Archaeological Trust

Parrington, M. (ed.) 1978 *The Excavation of an Iron Age Settlement, Bronze Age Ring Ditches and Roman Features at Ashville Trading Estate, Abingdon, Oxon. 1974–76* CBA Research Report **28**, London, Council for British Archaeology

Parry, C. 1999 'Iron-Age, Romano-British and medieval occupation at Bishop's Cleeve, Gloucestershire: excavations at Gilders Paddock 1989 and 1990–1', *Trans Bristol Gloucestershire Archaeol Soc* **117**, 89–118

Partridge, C. 1981 *Skeleton Green* Britannia Monograph Series **2**, London, Society for the Promotion of Roman Studies

Peacock, D.P.S. 1967 'Romano-British pottery production in the Malvern district of Worcestershire', *Trans Worcestershire Archaeol Soc* **1**, 15–29

Peacock, D.P.S. (ed.) 1977 *Pottery and Early Commerce: Characterisation and Trade in Roman and later Ceramics* London, Academic Press

Percival, J. 1921 *The Wheat Plant* London, Duckworth

Philpott, R. 1991 *Burial Practices in Roman Britain: A Survey of Grave Treatment and Furnishing AD 43–410* BAR British Series **219**, Oxford, British Archaeological Reports, 61–6

Postan, M. 1954 *The Famulus* Economic History Review Supplements **2**, London, Cambridge University Press

Rackham, J. (ed.) 1994 *Environment and Economy in Anglo-Saxon England* CBA Research Report **89**, London, Council for British Archaeology

Rawes, B. 1982 'Gloucester Severn Valley ware', *Trans Bristol Gloucestershire Archaeol Soc* **100**, 33–46
Rawes, B. and Rawes, B. 1989 'Stoke Orchard Road, The Grange, and Field Farm, Bishop's Cleeve', in B. Rawes (ed.) Archaeological Review 13, *Trans Bristol Gloucestershire Archaeol Soc* **107**, 253–4
Richardson, L. 1929 *The Country Around Moreton-in-Marsh. Explanation of Sheet 217, Memoir of the Geological Survey of England and Wales* London, HMSO
Robinson, M.A. 1979 'The biological evidence', in G. Lambrick and M.A. Robinson (eds), 77–133
Roe, F. 1993 'Worked stone', in A. Woodward and P. Leach, 197–201
Roe, F. 1998 'Worked stone', in A. Barber and G. Walker, 128–131
Roe, F. 1999 'The worked stone', in A. Mudd *et al.*, 414–21
Rogers, J. and Waldron, T. 1995 *A Field Guide to Joint Disease in Archaeology* Chichester, Wiley
Salter, C. 1998 'Metal-working debris', in A. Barber and G. Walker, 132–3
Smith, D.N. 1991 *An investigation of the potential of modern analogue faunas to act as comparisons to palaeoentomological samples from archaeological farm sites* unpublished Ph.D. thesis, University of Sheffield
Smith, D. N., Osborne, P.J. and Barrett, J. 1997 'Preliminary palaeoentomological research at the Iron Age site at Goldcliff, Gwent. 1991–1993', *Quaternary Proc* **5**, 255–67
Sobey, D.G. 1981 'Stellaria media', *J Ecol* **69**, 311–35
Stace, C. 1991 *New Flora of the British Isles* Cambridge, Cambridge University Press
Timby, J.R. 1998 *Excavations at Kingscote and Wycomb, Gloucestershire: A Roman Estate Centre and Small Town in the Cotswolds with Notes on Related Settlements* Cirencester, Cotswold Archaeological Trust
Timby, J. 1999 'The pottery', in A. Mudd *et al.*, 339–65
Tomber, R. and Dore, J. 1998 *The National Roman Fabric Reference Collection: A Handbook* London, Museum of London Archaeology Service/English Heritage/British Museum
Tottenham, C.E. 1954 *Coleoptera Staphylinidae. Section (a) Piestinae to Euaesthetinae* Handbooks for the Identification of British Insects **IV/8(a)**, London, Royal Entomological Society of London
Trotter, M. and Gleser, G.C. 1952 'Estimation of stature from long bones of American whites and Negroes', *American J Physical Anthropol* **10(4)**, 463–514
Trotter, M. and Gleser, G.C. 1957 'A re-evaluation of estimation of stature bases on measurements of stature taken during life and of long bones after death', *American J Physical Anthropol* **16(1)**, 79–123
Van Beek, G.C. 1983 *Dental Morphology: An Illustrated Guide* London & Boston, Wright PSG
Vince, A.G. 1977 'The medieval and post-medieval ceramic industry of the Malvern region: the study of a ware and its distribution', in D.P.S. Peacock (ed.), 257–306
Vince, A.G. 1983 'The medieval pottery', in C. Heighway, 125–61
Vince, A.G. 1986 'The pottery', in P. Ellis, 95–138
Viner, L. 1982 'The objects of bone, shale, clay, stone and lead', in J. Wacher. and A. McWhirr, 103–5
Wacher, J. and McWhirr, A. 1982 *Early Roman Occupation at Cirencester* Cirencester Excavations **I**, Cirencester, Cirencester Excavation Committee
Ward Perkins, J.B. 1967 *London Museum; Medieval Catalogue* London, HMSO

Webb, P.A.O. and Suchey, J.M. 1985 'Epiphyseal union of the anterior iliac crest and medial clavicle in a modern multiracial sample of American males and females', *American J Physical Anthropol* **68**, 457–66

Webster, P.V. 1976 'Severn Valley ware', *Trans Bristol Gloucestershire Archaeol Soc* **94**, 18–46

Webster, L. and Backhouse, J. 1991 *The Making of England: Anglo-Saxon Art and Culture AD 600–900* London, British Museum

Webster, G., Fowler, P., Noddle, B. and Smith, L. 1985 'The excavation of a Romano-British rural establishment at Barnsley Park, Gloucs. Part 3', *Trans Bristol Gloucestershire Archaeol Soc* **103**, 73–100

Wells, C. 1977 'Diseases of the maxillary sinus in antiquity', *Medical and Biological Illustration* **27**, 173–8

Wells, C. 1982 'The human burials', in A. McWhirr *et al.*, 135–202

Williams, D.F. 1977 'The Romano-British black-burnished industry: an essay on characterization by heavy mineral analysis', in D.P.S. Peacock (ed.), 163–220

Wilson, B., Grigson, C. and Payne, S. (eds) 1982 *Ageing and Sexing Animal Bones from Archaeological Sites* BAR British Series **109**, Oxford, British Archaeological Reports

Woodiwiss, S. (ed.) 1992 *Iron Age and Roman salt production and the medieval town of Droitwich* CBA Research Report **81**, London, Council for British Archaeology

Woodward, A. and Leach, P. 1993 *The Uley Shrines: Excavation of a Ritual Complex on West Hill, Uley, Gloucestershire 1977–9* English Heritage Archaeological Report **17**, London, English Heritage

Young, C.J. 1997 *Oxfordshire Roman Pottery* BAR British Series **43**, Oxford, British Archaeological Reports